TABOR COLLEGE LIBRARY
Hillsboro, Kansas 67063

CREATIVE WAYS TO PRESENT SCRIPTURE

D1469384

Word of Mouth

DATE DUE

Herald
Press

F&L
FAITH&LIFE
P R E S S

Winnipeg, Manitoba
Newton, Kansas

Waterloo, Ontario
Scottdale, Pennsylvania

Word of Mouth: Creative Ways to Present Scripture, by Ken Hawkley and Craig Morton, offers background, theory, and practical helps for oral presentation of Scripture, as well as 28 sample scripts for readers' theatre from the Gospel of John.

Copyright © 2000 by Faith & Life Press, Newton, Kansas. All rights reserved. Permission is granted by Faith & Life Press to photocopy the readers' theatre scripts in Part II only, for one-time use in the church congregation or group of the owner of this book. Otherwise, this publication may not be reproduced, stored in a retrieval system, or transmitted in whole or in part, in any form, by any means, electronic, mechanical, photocopying, recording, or otherwise, without prior permission of the copyright owners.

International Standard Book Number 0-87303-398-1

Unless otherwise noted, Scripture text used in this book, is from the New Revised Standard Version, copyright © 1989, Division of Christian education of the National Council of the Churches of Christ in the United States of America.

Cover and interior design: Nancy Miller

Printed in the United States of America

Table of Contents

INTRODUCTION

READERS' THEATRE SCRIPTS

TABOR COLLEGE LIBRARY
Hillsboro, Kansas 67063

Introduction

There is one drawback to having Scripture in written form: We have forgotten how to speak it. We hear it read out loud in church, but too often we hear little more than the words on a page. Sometimes readings from the pulpit are flat and lifeless. We tolerate them, because we think that as long as the words are conveyed, we should be getting the message.

There are other times, however, when a reader puts a great deal of time, talent, and practice into a presentation—and the Word comes alive and lodges in people's hearts. Sometimes, a Scripture-based readers' theatre opens new insights for a congregation. Those readers and worship planners have caught on what we want to convey in this book: The Bible is ripe for creative oral presentation! And the good news is that you don't need special talent to do it. If that were the case, we wouldn't be writing this book.

Much of our Bible, if not most, was transmitted orally long before it was written down. Back then there were the ancient storytellers, dramatizing the biblical stories with their expressive voices, strange antics, and peculiar gestures. Entrusted with the special task of remembering and passing on the great acts of God's faithfulness, they would tell the stories at festivals, in homes, around the fire, or on the banks of a wadi. Imagine the wonder on the faces of first-time hearers. Picture the expectation from those who knew what was going to happen next, or the contentment at hearing the familiar stories again, but with freshness for their lives.

Now imagine yourself as that storyteller, without all the dust, the heat, or the awful camel smells. In this book, we hope to help you tell the biblical story in a contemporary way, opening up the Scriptures as the oral presenters did in the old days, and with equal enthusiasm. We (Ken and Craig) have often been called simple, so we tried to keep that in mind when putting together this book. In the first part, we include four brief chapters

> The Bible is ripe for creative oral presentation! And the good news is that you don't need special talent to do it.

TABOR COLLEGE LIBRARY
Hillsboro, Kansas 67063

on the background and importance of oral interpretation, followed by practical helps on how to do it well. Then, we include several readers' theatre pieces from the Gospel of John, which illustrate some of what we've shared in the first part of the book. You are welcome to adapt these in your church setting, but we also hope you will use them as springboards for creating your own oral presentations of Scripture.

We believe the gathered people of God miss out when the Word is not told with the passion that the original people felt. Scripture is the Word of a living God, One who lives in us! It is our hope that through this resource, people may hear God's call anew, and be compelled to follow God in deeper ways. This is about the holy task of passing on the faith.

Acknowledgements

Thanks to the people of the Western District Conference of the General Conference Mennonite Church, who encouraged us to write and perform Scripture presentations. Thanks to the portion of the church that believes laughter in church is okay. Thanks also to our parents, who gave us the semblance of humor that we have. Thanks to the Commission on Education for supporting us in thinking, working, and writing together. And special thanks to Faith & Life Press for sticking its neck out on this project.

—*Ken Hawkley and Craig Morton*

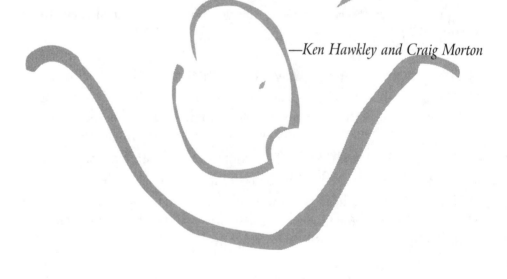

Chapter 1

From Og to Augsburger

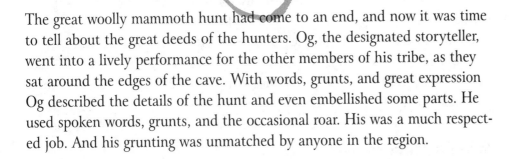

The great woolly mammoth hunt had come to an end, and now it was time to tell about the great deeds of the hunters. Og, the designated storyteller, went into a lively performance for the other members of his tribe, as they sat around the edges of the cave. With words, grunts, and great expression Og described the details of the hunt and even embellished some parts. He used spoken words, grunts, and the occasional roar. His was a much respected job. And his grunting was unmatched by anyone in the region.

When Og told a story, it stayed with the hearers, which, after all, was the whole point of the telling. Og was also a teacher of sorts, because he passed on traditions and ways of doing things that would help the tribe prosper. Og collected the beliefs and myths of the tribe as treasures to be repeated, so that people would believe the proper things and understand the rules of living. Og did all this through the spoken word.

Oral culture

Og is fictitious, but his position in prehistory is probably not. Og represents the earliest line of orators. He would have been the equivalent of storyteller, entertainer, priest, and teacher, rolled into one. His was a sacred task, and he was selected through special training or by evidence of a special gift. He may have been an elderly member of the tribe, having collected the old stories from the past into his memory. He was the one to link his tribe with the ancestors, heroes, trials, and triumphs of preceding generations. In a time when there was no paper, and when good cave walls were in short supply, the oral tradition was the most important way to pass on history, form identity, shape beliefs and worldviews, and supply a sense of belonging.

In order for the Hebrew people to understand that they were God's chosen people, it was important for histories and biographies to be passed on. Some scholars feel that the creation account of Genesis was constructed the way it was in order to answer questions children might ask, such as "How did we get here?" "Where do trees come from?" "Who named all the animals?" "Why are Mommy and Daddy shaped differently?" Later generations needed to know about the nature of God in order to worship God. Telling the

When Og told a story, it stayed with the hearers, which, after all, was the whole point of the telling.

history of God's acts and the biographies of God's chosen leaders was a way to pass on the reasons for respect, awe, fear, and hope that the people of God felt for their Creator.

Amazingly, that passing on happened largely by word of mouth. Biblical scholars feel certain that the first five books of the Bible (the Pentateuch or Torah for you sophisticates) existed orally for many hundreds of years before anything substantial was written down. In fact, most of the Bible is a compilation of stories, songs, prophecies, and other utterances that were heard more than they were read. Even the four gospels of the New Testament were based on the oral teachings and sayings of Jesus which, along with the stories, may not have been written down until decades after Jesus' resurrection. In the introduction of the Gospel of Luke, the writer clearly tells the reader that these things that he puts into an "orderly account" were passed on by eyewitnesses, probably over a period of years. And any reader of Luke and its companion, Acts, can experience the sense of immediacy that would have come in the oral retelling.

Modern studies of "primitive" tribes that still rely on oral culture reveal that stories, myths, and beliefs have been passed along through the generations with amazing consistency. Through their storytellers, they remember and pass on "facts" with accuracy. This may be hard for us moderns, dependent on paper and computers, to understand. Many of us have played the game Telephone, in which someone whispers a short story to another person, who passes it on to another and so on until everyone in the room has heard it from someone else. The last person then relates what he or she heard to the whole group. The results are hilarious because the story is so different from the original one. People from oral cultures would likely spoil the fun by passing on the story exactly as it was told to them. Party poopers they might be, but they are very well suited for maintaining cultural identity. Oral cultures pass along all the essential elements of themselves through their storytellers.

Stories and rituals

In the history of God's people, there has always been a strong pairing of our sacred stories and our rituals—those physical actions that help us commemorate important events and truths. To this day, in Jewish communities, the Passover ritual always includes stories of the Exodus from Egypt. The stories help explain what the ritual is about, why it is important, and that they belong to a special people, called by God. The stories reveal something of the nature of God and how God's people fit into God's plan for the world. These stories teach, give identity, and preserve sacred times as they are repeated throughout the generations.

Of course, this is also true of our own Christian rituals. Baptism, in many ways, is a reenactment of the story of Jesus, with whom the believer identifies. As a person publicly accepts Christ and begins the Christian life, the baptism ceremony recalls Jesus at the River Jordan. The story includes such moments as the descent of the Holy Spirit in the form of a dove, and the voice from the heavens saying: "This is my beloved son, in whom I am well pleased."

Communion likewise helps us retell our central story of Jesus' death and resurrection, reminding us of what we signed on for when we were baptized. When we take the bread and the cup we recall the Last Supper, where Jesus' spoke of giving his life for us. We also remember the promise, from Revelation, of the future heavenly "banquet" when Christ returns and all the nations will gather together to celebrate Christ's rule.

Foot washing, for many of us in the believers church tradition, is yet another ritual which unfolds before us as a story with drama. We picture the Last Supper, when Jesus washed the disciples' feet as a beautiful act of service. Testimonies and stories of reconciliation abound at such times, as indeed they should, for the ritual and the stories around it are about service and peacemaking.

Not only in the extraordinary rituals, but in ordinary times as well, story is central to our worship and to our faith. Story, oral tradition, and oral interpretation have played and continue to play an important role in the lives of faith communities. They let us know where we have come from, to whom we belong, and why. It is said that the tongue is the strongest muscle in the body. In the oral tradition, that is not surprising. The tongue must keep an entire people on the path toward their goal, upholding the past and pointing to the future.

Remember Og? Following those early days in prehistory, people's names got more sophisticated, and the things that were passed on from generation to generation became more and more complex. The caveman Og eventually gave way to modern orators with names like Augsburger.* But even with the invention of writing, paper, moveable type, romance novels, and now digital text, the spoken word holds a magic that cannot be duplicated. Especially in the church, it is right for us to venerate that oral tradition today, for it is in our spiritual heritage. Today our orators and speakers are still important for what they bring to our culture. In the church, they carry some of the same responsibilities as our fictitious caveman. The good ones inspire us and put us in touch with God and with ourselves, and teach us how we are to live.

Not only in the extraordinary rituals, but in ordinary times as well, story is central to our worship and to our faith. Story, oral tradition, and oral interpretation have played and continue to play an important role in the lives of faith communities. They let us know where we have come from, to whom we belong, and why.

* The name of a well-known speaker among Mennonites, Myron Augsburger. (The connection was used with his kind permission.)

9.

Chapter 2

A Very Brief History of Our Civilization
(And Why Oral Interpretation Is So Important Today)

Oral interpretation of Scripture at its best involves the whole person. It lures the imagination to consider the sounds, fragrances, tastes, and sights of a particular story or event. It helps us consider the social setting of a biblical story, including the emotional and spiritual aspects. Done right, it gets beyond having one head talk to another. The texts of our faith need to become events of faith that engage all of who we are—our bodies and our hearts, and not just our heads.

This way of thinking may seem revolutionary for those of us over 30 who were trained to think of the world in "head" terms. We are products of a culture greatly affected by the philosophy of the Enlightenment of the seventeenth and eighteenth centuries. The Enlightenment was a period in which the motto of the day was "I think, therefore I am." Believing that only reason made sense, people assumed that the mind, body, and spirit could be separated, and that the mind was the most important. Everything needed to be evaluated and proved by reason. It did not matter what your heart told you. Logic and the scientific method were all important.

This modern worldview, which has dominated Western civilization until very recently, produced unique and important contributions to science, exploration, medicine, physics, and culture. And not surprisingly, it affected the way people experienced their faith. The scientific approach to reality led to an explosion of scholarly work: studies on the history of Jesus, analysis of the claims of Christian faith, reasoned arguments about the validity of miracles, and a desire to reconcile the differing positions of orthodox Christian faith and modern thinking. The academic flurry helped Christians understand Scripture through the lens of first-century Palestine, and then translate its values into modern insights and application.

At the same time, however, much of Scripture was approached as a problem to be solved, rather than as a mystery to be explored. The price of the

Enlightenment's influence was that the simple narrative power of Scripture got further out of the reach of lay people. The new priest of the modern age was no longer the pastor but the scholar. Paul's insight that "faith comes from what is heard" (Rom. 10:17) became lost, as dissecting replaced telling and hearing.

The growing interest in creative oral interpretation of Scripture is a sign that a faith oriented primarily to the head is no longer acceptable in our post-modern age. Like the Hebrew culture from which the Bible sprang, we are realizing that we are called to experience our faith and our faith history in ways that involve the whole being. For the Hebrews, as for many other non-Western cultures today, the mind, the body, and the spirit are all connected in this thing we call a person. One of the Hebrew words for human beings, *nephesh*, encapsulates mind, spirit, life, heart, and vitality. In other words, a human being is a dynamic mix of feelings, thoughts, aches, and spiritual hunger all rolled into one synergistic package.

To be a human being means to experience, to reflect, and to feel. Words spoken and stories told touch us where we live. Who, upon hearing dreadful news, does not feel the weight of the words in the pit of their stomach? Who does not laugh (or groan) upon hearing a joke? Who has not cried or been physically moved at a movie? The point is that our communication involves our whole being. Listening with understanding, really hearing, leads not only to an intellectual but also to a physical response.

In approaching Scripture, therefore, we do not simply analyze its message with our left brain. While the methods of Bible study bequeathed to us by the modern era will continue to be important for us, and for the church, we must also give room for the creative impulses of the right brain to inform our experience of Scripture. That is why we (Craig and Ken) are so passionate about sharing this book with you.

The growing interest in creative oral interpretation of Scripture is a sign that a faith oriented primarily to the head is no longer acceptable in our post-modern age. Like the Hebrew culture from which the Bible sprang, we are realizing that we are called to experience our faith and our faith history in ways that involve the whole being.

Chapter 3
Dramatic Words Change the World

Human speech is both a gift and a curse. The gift is that the words we speak, hear, write, or read can be remembered. The curse is also that words can be remembered. Words are recalled, for good or ill, including our own! Sometimes I (Craig) think we'd be better off forgetting some words, such as the instructions on how to launch nuclear missiles, or what I said about my sister when I was a mad little kid. We know that others would be better off forgetting some of the things we have said. I'm sure you've said some dandies in you lifetime, too. But words also convey life, and these are the ones we want to remember. Words carry the stories that are so important to us. And the more dramatically they are told, the more we are likely to hear and remember their transforming message for us.

Beyond intellect

At the most basic level, words exist as spoken. Certainly there are words both read and written (and edited and rewritten). However, the words of speech existed long before an alphabet, before cuneiform, and before hiero-glyphic symbols. Think of the grunts of Og. What we spoke were the words narrating the passing of days and of generations. We retold epic tales of the tragedy of Adam and Eve, of the journey of Noah, and of the faithful sojourn of Abraham and Sarah. Before these epic stories were written, these events were told and retold. But not as a news report on the evening news, purporting to be only the empirical and objective facts. These stories also carried emotion, spiritual meaning, and insight into human striving. These words spoke to life, with all its ups and downs.

Words, finely considered, communicate to more than what we narrowly call intellect. Carrying more than raw data, words speak to the heart and spirit, as well as to the mind. Some words even affect our bodies. Whisper the name "Dracula" in a dark room on a stormy night, and actually feel the effect of the word. Or feel the splash of joy that may come with the words "pay day" immediately deflated as we sneer three letters, "IRS."

While facts convey a degree of the story, they cannot do justice to reality. The development of the media illustrates this well. Until television, a radio report had to convey the totality of the environment: the smells, the sights, the emotions of those present. The place given to the imagination, guided by the reporters' firsthand accounts, led to some of the most memorable journalism of the twentieth century. The drama, not just the facts, was presented.

At one time in my preaching career I was told not to tell stories. What was needed, I was told, was more "facts." This criticism assumed that the more verifiable, "scientific" information we get, the better off we will be. As we saw in the last chapter, the trap of this modern view of life is that the emotions, as well as the more tactile, bodily ways of knowing are given short shrift. For human beings to be fully human means to speak and read words which not only point out the breadth of human experience, but in the telling and hearing bring the whole of the person to the event.

An event, not just a text

We humans like dramatic events that bring something new into our lives and leave us changed. There is probably more drama in our lives than we realize. Some drama unfolds during a conversation over coffee. Some dramas, like a marriage, unfold over decades. These dramas are events — sometimes filled with laughter, sometimes with groaning. But we like seeing them acted out because they tell us something about our life experience. Stories well told stir empathy. Such dramas bring common ground to diverse people.

Interviewed about his work as a screenwriter for the movie, *Shakespeare in Love*, British playwright Tom Stoppard shared his intrigue with Shakespeare. About his "first deep" experiences of seeing *Hamlet*, Stoppard said, "It alerted you… It jumped you into the central truth about theatre, which is that it is an event, not a text'" (*Time*, January 25, 1999). Words carry meaning not only in the dictionary sense, but also in the course of events that the words share with you and me. Drama extends beyond the text and grabs you. You are there.

Written words point into the world of the reader, penetrating the boundary between the reader and the writer. That boundary can be made even more permeable, however, when the words are taken from a page and spoken to hearers, not just readers. That's what we try to do with our oral interpretations of Scripture. Through oral presentation–soliloquy, dialogue, poetry, rhetoric–words carry drama. Drama occurs when the words reach out to

Before these epic stories were written, these events were told and retold. But not as a news report on the evening news, purporting to be only the empirical and objective facts. These stories also carried emotion, spiritual meaning, and insight into human striving. These words spoke to life, with all its ups and downs.

impress upon one's spirit the whole spectrum of what is heard. And as art it resists being pigeonholed and defined into one meaning. Instead, meaning expands and becomes complex and addresses many questions. In good drama, there are as many questions as there are hearers.

Drama transforms

In the complexities and questions lies transformation. Whether the drama is about history or about daily life, whether it is funny or sad, adventuresome or even mundane, watching a theatrical performance transforms us. Drama, as an event, signifies a new experience. As a new experience it builds upon old information with new information. Experience transforms into knowledge as it is incorporated into life.

Because we experience it, the drama becomes a new firsthand event, leaving us with decisions to make. Does this reflect my values? Did I understand the motivation of any of the characters? What would I be like in the same situation? These and similar questions draw the story into our lives, and our lives into drama. We are changed. Our sense of identity grows.

Nowhere does this happen more profoundly than when we use the biblical story as the source for drama. That is one of the reasons we offer this book to those who want to bring Scripture to life in the church. By entering into the Scripture as drama, by hearing the Bible as more than words on a page that speak to our intellect, and by allowing the dynamic event of the story or text to speak to our whole being, we open ourselves to the transforming power of God's words. To experience Scripture, not simply read it, is a part of the personal transformation God seeks in creating a people.

Drama occurs when the words reach out to impress upon one's spirit the whole spectrum of what is heard. And as art it resists being pigeonholed and defined into one meaning. Instead, meaning expands and becomes complex and addresses many questions. In good drama, there are as many questions as there are hearers.

Chapter 4
Oral Interpretation Builds Community

A readers' theatre or some other form of oral interpretation involves eyes, ears, and mouth. Into the ears go two basic things—sounds and Q-tips. Of these two, the sounds are powerful in forming our ideas and our character. The cotton swabs merely keep our ears clean enough to enjoy the sonic experience. Eyes are witnesses driven by instinct, interest, and desire. Mouths are more problematic. Out of the mouth can come all kinds of stuff–some of it sweet, thoughtful, and refreshing, and some of it harsh, tasteless, and stupid. But between the ears and behind the eyes resides the brain, which makes meaning out of all the input. This organ of gray matter also tries to help the mouth make a meaningful contribution. (Of course, sometimes it instructs us to just plug our ears, close our eyes, and shut up.)

Holes in our heads

The remarkable thing is that these holes in our head help create community. In fact, community is a compilation of people with holes in their heads. Community is formed out of sharing common beliefs, languages, fashions, appetites, political interests, religious convictions, experiences, and values—things that are communicated through our mouths, eyes, and ears. And everyone is in some kind of community. As the poet John Donne wrote, "No man is an island, entire of himself." To be human means to share community with others, either by intention (such as the church), by location (one's street or apartment block), or seemingly by accident (a planeload of people, stranded on the runway).

In sharing Scripture with our mouths, we project to another's ears (and through props to their eyes as well) an interpretation of a sacred text. In the oral presentation, the speaker interprets the text by adding emotion, accent, rhythm, and cadence. In the simple act of presentation, a character is created. This character—be it John the Baptist (John 1), the woman at the well (John 4), or Nicodemus (John 3)—becomes a living person for a time, taken from history and reintroduced afresh. When a reader, writer, or speaker, presents a Scripture text, the biblical character enters into a community of

When a reader, writer, or speaker, presents a Scripture text, the biblical character enters into a community of faith, and that community will test this character to determine his or her relevance to its life.

faith, and that community will test this character to determine his or her relevance to its life.

Creativity brings tension

The exercise of hearing an ancient speaker in new and surprising ways creatively stretches our understanding of our faith. At the same time, it can bring tension to a community. One type of tension originates in the manner of storytelling, whether through unconventional gestures or tones of voice, or the way one tries to put a contemporary spin on a scriptural character or story. There are times when I cannot look at the audience for fear of being speared by their unease. They don't know if they like what they hear, or if they will be helped by it. Yet the desire to find out often forces them to stay and listen, or look around and try to figure things out.

Humor can also contribute to the tension, especially when it is not funny for everyone. Humor, sometimes defined as the art of finding opposites, causes unease when it allows the unexpected to arise to the consciousness by means of the unconscious. Sometimes, for example, the words sound right, but the meaning is confused, surprising, or ironic. In his book *Intent on Laughter*, humorist John Bailey writes, "To put emphasis in the wrong place means that there is a non-emphasis where the emphasis should be and it is therefore an opposite."

Emphasizing what is regularly overlooked and de-emphasizing the more apparent provides a surprise. The presentation then becomes not so much another piece of processed information as a firsthand experience of an event leading to new awareness for both the hearer and the teller. Even if the hearers do not laugh, good humor will help awaken insight. We hope this is your experience as you use our readers' theatre pieces from the Gospel of John.

Finally, tension comes from the suspense we create in the act of storytelling. Try telling someone part of a story. As you approach the climax, just stop telling and walk away, or change the topic. Even if it's a ho-hum story, most people will be unhappy with you. It is because the story got to the point of tension, and left the tension unresolved. Unfinished stories make people grumpy. When a story is performed, recited, or told, the hearers get pleasantly stuck in this tension. They are willing to suspend their judgment and be ushered into another "realm" mentally. They are in Galilee seeing Jesus by the sea, or they are in the upper room afraid to breathe for fear of missing a word. They want to know how it will end.

Tension is good

Oral interpretation will bring both personal tension, and tension within the community. But that can be a healthy thing. Psychiatrist M. Scott Peck says community without tension would be considered dead. To be alive means to exist in tension. "Every living organism ... whether a cat or a human being, exists in tension between sleeping and waking, rest and exercise... and so on. For a community to continue to exist, it also must live in ongoing tension. We humans hunger for genuine community and will work hard to maintain it precisely because it is the way to live most fully, most vibrantly. Being the most alive of entities, true communities must consequently pay the price of experiencing even more tension than other organizations" (*The Different Drum: Community Making and Peace*).

So let the oral interpretation begin. Let the hearers suspend their judgment as the presenters recreate the biblical scene for them. Let the hearers react to the words used to retell the story. Let them process how it made them feel to see Mary speak to the gardener that day, or how it felt to hear the voice of Jesus raise Lazarus from the grave. Let them bring their own emotions to the story. As the story begins to interact with the gathered hearers, a new level of community is attained by many of those who shared this moment together. Just as dramatic words lead to personal transformation, they also lead to change and growth within our communities of faith.

Chapter 5
Steps and Techniques: Practical pointers for effective presentation of Scripture

We have waxed passionately about the important place that oral interpretation of Scripture should have in our faith communities. Have we convinced you by now that it is the best thing since fire? We hope so. Now it's time to get practical. In this chapter we want to give you some pointers on how to plan and present your oral interpretation effectively. The pointers we offer apply to presentations that are dramatic in some sense, whether it is reading the text dramatically from the Bible, or interpreting the text through readers' theatre. Our sample scripts that follow fit the latter category. However, many of these guidelines apply also to traditional Scripture readings, done by a single reader.

Choose your setting

There are many places and events where oral interpretation of Scripture can enrich our church life and our growth in faithfulness. Worship services are likely the first event to come to mind. But Bible study, Sunday school, church retreats, vacation Bible school, and evangelistic events are also great venues. Some less traditional settings include committee meetings, congregational business meetings, youth rallies, potluck meals, family devotions, or the openings and closings of service projects. Tasteful and appropriate dramatizations of Scripture can enhance weddings, baptisms, membership covenants, and even funerals. In fact, just about anywhere and anytime that Scripture is referred to can be an opportunity to tell the Scripture through oral interpretation.

Select the text

It is important to select a biblical text that suits the event. In many worship settings, the choice is made for you by the planners, whether they follow the

> Just about anywhere and anytime that Scripture is referred to can be an opportunity to tell the Scripture through oral interpretation.

lectionary schedule or another plan. However, it is important that both the choice of text and your style of presentation fit the mood and theme of the event. If someone else will be the main presenter at an event, be sure to learn from that person how he or she intends to use the biblical text. Remember that oral presentation is not window dressing, or pure entertainment. It should be integrated into the other parts of the event, reinforcing the theme.

If it is up to you to choose the text, you will need to set the limits of the text, and that can be a difficult decision. How much of it will you present? Where will you begin and where will you end? That depends on several factors. Time will be one consideration. Keep in mind that Scripture presentation is not usually expected to take much time in a worship event, so long passages of two or three chapters will in most cases be ruled out. Also keep in mind that some oral presentations take longer than a straight reading of the text. Our scripts show that that "scenic route" may indeed take longer.

If you are a beginner, use biblical passages that are easiest to tell or dramatize as stories. Remember that our faith is grounded in the stories, and stories communicate better than didactic forms of communication. Put on the shoes of the characters, study the background of the text and the setting, and bring them to life for those who hear.

The purpose of the oral presentation will also influence the boundaries of the Scripture passages. You will want to focus as narrowly as possible on a single point, theme, or insight that relates most directly to the theme and needs of the event. If you have a lengthy passage, consider what can be left out. Which parts of the passage relate directly to what you wish to say and which parts do not? Oral interpretation requires a certain economy of material chosen, so don't be afraid to cut, remaining focused on your theme and purpose.

Write your script

One reason why you purchased this book was probably for the scripts we created from the Gospel of John. They are for you to use, and we hope they are helpful. You may find other scripts on the market that may help you enhance your worship experiences. But we also encourage you to write your own. In doing so, keep the following principles in mind:

Make sure the Scripture fits. Again, make sure there is correspondence between the point of the event (the coming sermon, the Bible study, the ceremony, etc.), and the point of your script.

Be creative in introducing your characters. The weakest way is to have the characters introduce themselves in an unnatural way. Beginning the oral presentation with, "Hi, I'm Pontius Pilate," is not a natural way for people to speak.

Use humor appropriately. Humor is often used to lighten the mood and draw people into the content of the text. When it is used just before a serious point is made, the contrast can heighten the power of that point. Humor can also be used to invite people to see things differently. But humor is also a delicate matter, and depends greatly on the context and the audience. It can distract from the point, or worse, offend the people listening. Be careful not to make fun of Scripture. In our scripts we try to make fun of life and of the foibles inherent in us all, but not the Scripture itself.

Be prepared to write and rewrite. It goes with the territory. In writing your own scripts, the best tool is a person who will honestly critique your work. If that person has some training or experience in oral presentation and drama, you've hit the jackpot!

Present your script

When you have a script in hand—whether one of your own, one of ours, or someone else's—it is now important to present it effectively. To do that, you will need some preparation. Here are a few tips.

Practice makes smooth. Memorization is often ideal, but for most settings it will not be practical to expect participants to know the scripts by heart. Most of our scripts will present well if the participants have their scripts in hand; they are designed as "readers' theatre." However, things will not go well if there has been no practice. Go over the script enough to know the gist of what is being said. Once you think you know the sequence of things, read and practice it some more.

Mind your "P's." That is, know when to pause. In our scripts, pauses are written in where we think they should go. Pauses signify a change in action, place, time, or mood. But there may also be unscheduled pauses. One of those times would come if there is laughter. You should read the script and know where to expect laughter. If you speak through the laughter, people will miss your line.

In our scripts we try to make fun of life and of the foibles inherent in us all, but not the Scripture itself.

Sometimes your pauses will be long enough to sound like deep silences. Silence might be effective just before the climax or "punch line" to build suspense or to emphasize the last line of the presentation. In this latter case, silence and a freeze in your posture will be enough for the audience to know that this is a time to ponder.

Use pauses with confidence, but always have a good reason for doing so. Used well, they are powerful. Be cautious, however, not to overuse them. Know your cues. When there are multiple parts, know when your part is coming up so that there isn't an uncomfortable pause while your partners are trying to telepathically tell you to pay attention! Know what the person says just before you speak and listen for that cue during the presentation. Highlight your lines directly on the script. Also, make any production changes on the script.

Know what to do when you are speaking, and when you are not. If you are the one speaking, make sure you are turned to the audience, so they can hear you. If the script calls for you to look at another presenter while you speak, make sure they are reasonably placed so that the audience can hear you. Keep in mind that a slight turn in another's direction can be as effective as actually turning to that person, at least in a dramatic presentation.

When you are not speaking, assume a neutral pose. Stop movement and either look down, at the audience, or toward the one speaking. Keep your head still and maintain a stance that won't have you swaying back and forth like a metronome.

Plan your staging. In general, readers' theatre requires little movement around the stage. However, where you stand can either help or hinder the presentation. In most cases, the presenters should stand relatively close together. In others, there may be a good case for separation of one or more characters. If two people are engaged in a dialogue, for example, they might step forward from the group. Other groupings or separation may be appropriate to the mood or setting of the text. If any movement is made, it is best done during a pause in speech, so that the speech is not lost.

Look up. When it is your turn to speak, look up at the audience for at least the first few words.(Of course, sometimes you will be speaking to another character on stage, in which case you would, of course, look at him or her.) This helps to maintain audience participation and interest. If you have a longer speech, look up as often as you can. Eye contact will keep the listeners with you. If eye contact scares you, simply look over everyone's head at something in the back of the room.

Eye contact will keep the listeners with you. If eye contact scares you, simply look over everyone's head at something in the back of the room.

21.

Breathe well. Breath control during regular conversation is natural for us. In front of an audience, however, we seem to forget how to breathe properly and our anxiety may leave us short of breath. Before you begin, practice breathing deeply and regularly from the diaphragm, drawing air in through the nose and out through the mouth. As you rehearse your piece, be conscious of places where you need to breathe and mark those places on the script, if necessary. Proper breath control can aid in preventing your voice from dropping at the end of clauses and sentences.

Breathing can also help to punctuate your oral interpretation. Taking a breath at the end of the sentence will not only tell listeners that a thought is finished, it will allow them a brief moment to take in what was said. There may also be dramatic pauses where you stop to take a deep breath or two. This may serve as a good way to move from one emotion to another, for instance. A new breath at the beginning of a sentence will also allow you to speak loudly enough for people to hear you.

Enunciate. In informal conversation, we all slur words. In public presentations, however, it is crucial that we enunciate clearly, and in a way that the speech is not stilted or artificial. Concentrate on the consonants and the endings of words and phrases. Practice enunciation until you can do so at near normal conversation speed.

Before you perform your piece, warm up your tongue and your lips by reading the piece aloud, overemphasizing syllables, or by singing. Another good exercise is to repeat tongue twisters as fast as possible with accuracy. Here are a few to try:

Toy boat.

A big black bug bit a big black bear and made the big black bear bleed.

Unique New York.

Red leather, yellow leather.

Get the speed right. Seldom is any oral piece so one-dimensional that a single speed will suffice. Pronouncing certain words more slowly adds emphasis to those words. Faster speech may provide a more upbeat or excited mood, while slower speech may provide a more somber mood. In your practicing, vary the rate at which you speak, according to the emotions you are trying to portray. If you are portraying more than one character, use speed variations to help the audience differentiate between the characters

Pay attention to volume and pitch. You can shout for joy or out of anger, but loudness is only one element of conveying the proper emotion. Sometimes a whisper gets the point across more effectively than a shout. In order to get the volume and pitch right for you, think about how your voice behaves when you are joyful, angry, sad, confused, etc. Use your own natural voice in these circumstances as a basis for portraying these emotions in your presentation.

Use emphasis and tone. Decide which parts of sentences or words to emphasize. Be choosy, however, because stressing too many parts can make the presentation sound too melodramatic or lacking in focus. Emphasis can change meaning. For example, consider the question, "What did you do?" Emphasizing different words and using different volume and pitch can give the question many interpretations. Pitch, volume, and emphasis work together to help create the mood of your piece. Using the proper tone at the proper time can enhance the drama of a given piece.

Use gestures. The key physical gestures in oral interpretation are facial expressions. These must be "larger" than normal, if you want people to see them. More subtle facial expressions will not be noticed. If the audience is too large, facial expressions of any sort will not be very effective.

Use other physical gestures only if the piece calls for it. Remember that gestures are aids to get the point across; they should not distract from your oral presentation. Gestures should be simple and definite. For instance, pounding a surface once is more effective than repeatedly banging on the surface. Carefully consider whether a gesture is just an add-on or whether it actually does enhance the presentation. Practice your gestures so that you are comfortable with them. Make sure they are consistent with the mood and meaning you wish to convey.

Sometimes a whisper gets the point across more effectively than a shout. In order to get the volume and pitch right for you, think about how your voice behaves when you are joyful, angry, sad, confused, etc.

Readers' Theatre Scripts
from the Gospel of John

Permission Notice

Permission is granted by Faith & Life Press to photocopy these scripts for one-time use in the congregation or group of the owner of this book. Any other reproduction is a violation of copyright.

1. The Word

John 1:1-5, 10-18

As John begins his Gospel story he is concerned to clarify that Jesus Christ existed before the creation of the world. But the specificity with which John tries to do this can leave heads spinning at times. In fact, John is closing the loopholes that would allow anyone to disregard or minimize Jesus' identity.

READER 1	In the beginning was the word.
READER 2	And what was it?
READER 1	Pardon?
READER 2	The word! What was it?! Let's hear what the word was.
READER 1	If you'll wait, I'll tell you.
READER 2	Shall we guess?
READER 1	NO! [*pause*] In the beginning was the Word, and the Word was…
READER 2	[*makes drumroll sound*]
READER 1	…with God, and the word was God.
READER 2	Hold it!
READER 1	Must you interrupt?
READER 2	Well, yes, there's mistake in the Bible.
READER 1	Where?
READER 2	It clearly says, "In the beginning was the Word."
READER 1	Correct.
READER 2	Indicating only one word.
READER 1	[*uncertain where this is leading, but smelling a trap*] Yeah. Well…
READER 2	But the Word was with God, and the Word was God? That's confusing and inaccurate. Which is it—is it *with* or *was*? It has to be one or the other. Either the word they talk about was *with* God, or it *was* God.
READER 1	It is.
READER 2	But…
READER 1	The Word is God.
READER 2	What's with God?
READER 1	That's what I am trying to explain.
READER 2	I still don't get it.
READER 1	The Word is Jesus Christ.
READER 2	Now we have three names! Are we talking about "with," "was," or "Jesus"?
READER 1	Look, the Word was with God.

Production Notes

Participants: *Two readers*

A quick wit and a rhythm will help this readers' theater piece move. Many of the statements are short and quick. There may be times of laughter, so let the chuckles subside a bit before reading the next line.
Reader 2 carries the piece with inquisitive questions, asked innocently, not in an accusatory or critical tone. Reader 1 will at times become exasperated and a bit confused.

READER 2	Oh, we're back to that.
READER 1	But the Word is Jesus Christ
READER 2	Not with God?
READER 1	Most certainly with God.
READER 2	Could we go on until my head clears?
READER 1	He was in the beginning with God.
READER 2	Who's "he"?
READER 1	Jesus Christ.
READER 2	How did he get into this?
READER 1	It's his story.
READER 2	So Jesus Christ was with God at the beginning.
READER 1	Yes, all things came into being and without him not one thing came into being.
READER 2	What?
READER 1	Life has come into being through him and the life was a light for everyone.
READER 2	He created life?
READER 1	Right!
READER 2	Jesus Christ?
READER 1	The Word!
READER 2	Not Jesus Christ?
READER 1	Most certainly…
1 & 2	…with God.
READER 1	He was in the world and the world came into being through him.
READER 2	Who's he? God? Or Jesus? Or the Word?
READER 1	Yes.
READER 2	Which?
READER 1	He's just one.
READER 2	The Word?
READER 1	Jesus Christ.
READER 2	Not the Word?
READER 1	Most certainly…
1&2	…with God.
READER 2	I'm still not getting this. He, whoever that is, was in the world and then the world came into being?
READER 1	No, he was in the world, but the world did not know him.
READER 2	It's no wonder, he keeps changing.
READER 1	He came into what was his own, but his own people did not accept him.
READER 2	The Word?

READER 1   Jesus Christ…

READER 2   …with God.

1&2   But to all who received him, who believed in his name, he gave them the power to become children of God.

READER 2   To all who believed in his name?

READER 1   Yes, Jesus Christ.

READER 2   But he was not *The Word*?

READER 1   Most certainly he was.

READER 2   But how do you know which name…

READER 1   You just said it.

READER 2   The Word, right?

READER 1   Jesus Christ.

1&2   With God.

READER 1   All who believed were born of God.

READER 2   Could we go back to beginning?

READER 1   That's where we are.

READER 2   In the beginning?

READER 1   Was the Word.

READER 2   [*expectantly*] And the word was…?

READER 1   With God, and the Word was God.

READER 2   [*deflated and defeated*] This Bible stuff is difficult.

—K.H.

2. What Are You Looking At?

John 1:29-39a

When John came to baptize Jesus, he was a rugged picture of a prophet, with rough clothes and no-nonsense words. Standing in the Jordan River, John baptized those seeking to wash away the sins of the past. The baptism that John performed was different from baptism in the early church in that John's was a purification rite in preparation for the coming of the Messiah. Throughout Jesus' ministry, the Gospel writer refers to the identity of John and the meaning of his ministry as the forerunner of Jesus. Watching John and taking him seriously, we discover Jesus.

Production Notes

Participants: *John and two bystanders*

John is dressed roughly in work clothes, and stands at one side of the stage. You may wish to have him baptizing people in pantomime. The bystanders are at the other side. They use binoculars as they watch John from some distance. (Toilet paper tube binoculars work fine.)

BYSTANDER 1   What are you looking at?

BYSTANDER 2   Who, me?

BYSTANDER 1   Yeah, you.

BYSTANDER 2   If you hang around this river long enough, you'll see almost anything. People have been parading through here for the past week, all just to get a bath.

BYSTANDER 1   There are other places to get a bath. It must be a promotional for new deodorant soap.

BYSTANDER 2   Could be, but who needs this bug-eating lunatic giving you a bath? He's out there talking to the clouds and shouting away, and then mumbling, then kersplash, he gets you all wet. The whole city's been coming out. Even the hoity-toity types. I saw a lady get her peacock-feathered hat drenched by that dunker.

BYSTANDER 1   Hey, who's that?

BYSTANDER 2   I hear somebody yelling about sheep. Oh, no, those sheep are gonna mess in the water. And you know how bad wet wool smells.

BYSTANDER 1   It's not that clean after all these bathers, anyway.

JOHN   Here is the Lamb of God.

BYSTANDER 2   A "lamb"? Of God?

BYSTANDER 1   He's a funny looking lamb. No wool, good!

BYSTANDER 2   That's not a lamb, it's a man.

BYSTANDER 1   I didn't think he looked like a lamb. But he said it was a lamb!

BYSTANDER 2	We're too far to hear. Maybe he said, "a fan of God," or the Spam of God.
BYSTANDER 1	God doesn't eat Spam. I think he did say "Lamb."
1&2	Hmmm….
JOHN	This is he of whom it is said, "After me comes a man who ranks ahead of me because he was before me." I myself did not know him; but I came baptizing with water for this reason, that he might be revealed to Israel.
BYSTANDER 2	He's been eating bad grasshoppers! After you, or ahead of you. Make up your mind!
BYSTANDER 1	Shhhhhh. Did he say "repealed," or… [*cuts off in mid sentence, by a surprise*] Aah… you didn't see that, did you?
BYSTANDER 2	You mean that white thing?
BYSTANDER 1	[*nods in affirmation*]
BYSTANDER 2	No I didn't see it either. And I did not see it land on him.
BYSTANDER 1	Good, neither did I. What we did not see, it didn't look like a bird flying down, did it?
BYSTANDER 2	Yup, I did not see the white dove, you mean, land on him. It was his shoulder it landed on that we didn't see, right?
BYSTANDER 1	Ah, yeah.
	[*The next day. Signify this with a sign, or an announcement from off stage.*]
BYSTANDER 1	What are you looking at?
BYSTANDER 2	Who me?
BYSTANDER 1	Yeah you.
BYSTANDER 2	It's the bug guy again.
BYSTANDER 1	The bug guy? We just had the shack sprayed last week, we don't need him yet.
BYSTANDER 2	No, the guy who eats bugs.
BYSTANDER 1	Oh, him. Still giving baths, is he?
BYSTANDER 2	Not today, he's talking with his disciples.
BYSTANDER 1	Hey, here comes that guy who we did not see the dove land on.
	[*both turn, as if to follow*]
JOHN	Behold, here is the Lamb of God!
BYSTANDER 2	You know, he's not saying "Islam-abad," or the "land of nod," he said…
BYSTANDER 1	Behold, here is the Lamb of God.

BYSTANDER 2	I wonder what he means. I wonder what he's here for.
BYSTANDER 1	I wonder where the dove went.
BYSTANDER 2	You really saw it?
BYSTANDER 1	Yeah. You too?
BYSTANDER 2	Yeah.
BYSTANDER 1	Look, they're leaving with him—with the lamb guy.
BYSTANDER 2	I wonder where he's going. I wonder where he staying.
BYSTANDER 1	I wonder if we can follow.
BYSTANDER 2	I wonder if…
JOHN	[*motioning to them*] Come. Come. Come and see.

—C.M.

3. Clean Your Room!
John 2:13-22

This is a lighter approach to the story of the cleansing of the temple. As with other scripts, the humor is meant to help the audience think about the story from a new perspective.

READER 1	Jesus must have been a terrible child.
READER 2	How so?
READER 1	Can you imagine asking him to clean his room?
READER 2	Say more.
READER 1	Well, it was Passover, and Jesus and his disciples entered the temple.
READER 2	THE temple
READER 1	The TEMPLE
READER 2	The HOLY temple
READER 1	And people were selling goats and sheep and cattle and doves.
READER 2	And key chains and sunglasses and commemorative spoons and those pens that when you hold them upright the camel slides between the pyramid and the river.
READER 1	And there were money changers there too
READER 2	Trading dinars for denarii [*pronounced "deenars" and "denaree"*].
READER 1	The noise was deafening.
READER 2	HARDLY a place of worship.
READER 1	More like the trading floor of the New York Stock Exchange.
READER 2	A little like trying to worship in the middle of Toronto airport [*substitute a large airport near you*]
READER 1	So Jesus decided enough was enough.
READER 2	And enough was too much
READER 1	He cleaned house.
READER 2	He formed a whip of cords and drove out the sheep and cattle.
READER 1	He threw money around like it was chicken feed, and threw chicken feed around like it was...well, you get the point.
READER 2	Tables were upset.
READER 1	To say nothing of the people.
READER 2	And the sheep and the cows.

Production Notes

Participants: *Two readers*

This script is often fast-paced, intended to leave people a bit breathless. It will need enough rehearsal to give the two readers ease with the flow and pace, allowing lines to follow after one another without hesitation.

READER 1	The stampede alone held up traffic for hours.
READER 2	So leaders of the temple asked, "Do you have a permit for temple cleansing?"
READER 1	And Jesus said, "That's nothing, tear down this temple and I'll raise it up in three days."
READER 2	But Jesus was not talking about the TEMPLE
READER 1	THE temple
READER 2	But he meant the temple of his body.
READER 1	And no one knew what in the world he was talking about.
READER 2	Until he died and was raised again in three days.
READER 1	So how come its called CLEANSING the temple when Jesus made such a mess?
READER 2	A point to ponder.
READER 1	But a warning to the children here.
READER 2	[*pause, wag your finger at the audience*] Don't try this at home.

—K.H.

4. Your Life Is Ajar
John 4:1-30, 39-42

This is a piece about a woman with a jar, at a well. The "jar" for all of us is those things we do repeatedly to seek fulfillment, but they can easily become compulsive, addictive, and deadly to body and soul. Our life can never satisfy us when we fill our own jars, but only when the God-shaped space in us becomes filled with the Living Water of God.

Every day
The same well
The same thirst
The same jug
Every day.
[*pause*]
The jug upon my head, I walk back.
At home, the coolness of the water soothes
The throat, the skin.
We live.
[*pause*]
But every day the same walk
To the same well
For the same thirst
With the same jug.
Every day the thirst is there from the day's awakening
To the night's farewell to the light.
[*pause*]
And every day
To the same well
By the same path
With the same jug.
[*pause*]
Who is this Jew
Asking me to give him a drink?
A sinner, a vagrant, someone lost?
A rabbi?
[*pause*]
But he asked for the water.
He asked me to serve him from Jacob's well.
From the same well

Production Notes

Participants: *Single actor, a woman*

A necessary prop for this script is an earthen jar or ceramic jug, the larger and heavier the better. If possible, have a tub filled with water, hidden by a wall of bricks or stones. The sound of trickling water as the woman ladles it from the well, would add a great deal to the piece, since it touches a deep instinctive chord in the human spirit. If possible, the woman should begin the monologue as she walks up to the well. She should walk slowly, not trudging, but like she is tired of the monotony of the walk. During the first part, she should use body language that expresses her feelings of internal shame and unworthiness. As the piece continues, her countenance lifts. As she leaves at the end, the change is one of obvious energy and joy.

For a similar thirst
From this jug.
[*pause*]
From water to thirst
From thirst to "living water," he said.
Parched
Bleak
Empty
Barren
He knew things no one else knows.
We talked about husbands and mountain
And worship and Messiah.
[*pause*]
The same well
By the same path
To the same water
With the same jug.
[*pause*]
The same jug
It always goes empty
I always return as thirsty as before.
His first words were, "Give me a drink."
Now my thirst is broken.
[*pause*]
I leave my jug by the well. [*Having set the jar down by the well, she begins to walk a tentative step away. She hesitates to walk away further.*]
[*pause*]
It's not the same water
Not the same path
Not the same well.
[*pause*]
I leave my jug at the well. [*This time she says this almost as a confession of faith, a conviction, but still is standing only a step away. She turns back and points to the jug to deliver her line.*]
[*pause*]
I left my jug at the well. [*As she exits the stage, perhaps several yards away, half way down a center aisle, or from the left or right edge of the stage, she points back with dignity, faith, and hope.*]

—C.M.

5. From the Place Where He Lives

John 4:46-54

In this story of the healing of an official's son, Jesus is found to be capable of healing from a distance. However, one really has to question whether Jesus is really that far away at all. What is in the heart of the official? He already has identified Jesus as one capable of helping and healing his son. What if Jesus lives in the heart of those who trust him? Then Jesus is close and present in very real ways.

READER 1	I'm going to tell you a Bible story, and feel free to ask questions if you don't understand. Understand?
READER 2	Sure.
READER 1	This is about a trip Jesus made to Cana, a village in Galilee, not far from his hometown.
READER 2	Can I ask a question?
READER 1	I haven't even begun, really. What don't you understand?
READER 2	I thought Jesus' hometown was in heaven.
READER 1	Well it was. But this was his other hometown.
READER 2	How many hometowns did he have?
READER 1	Oh, three or four, but that's really beside the point, let's get back to the story. You see, Jesus had come back to the town where he had turned water into wine.
READER 2	What kind of wine? Did they smell the corks and have fancy waiters bring...
READER 1	[*interrupting*] Excuse me! That's all beside the point. LET me go on [*deep sigh*]. So, Jesus was in Cana, where he had done something with stuff people drank [*looking sternly at reader 2*]—don't say anything!—and he met a royal official whose son was sick.
READER 2	And the son was sick in bed in Capernaum, right?
READER 1	[*surprised*] Yes—how did you know? [*resumes*] This man ran and begged Jesus, "Come and heal my son."
READER 2	"Heal your son?" Jesus said, "Must you see signs and wonders before you believe?"
READER 1	Then the official said to Jesus, "Sir, come to my home before my son dies."
READER 2	I have a question! [*The younger reader begins to rise.*]

Production Notes

Participants: *Two readers*

In their repartee, the two readers establish a relationship akin to that of teacher and student. Reader 2 should be a child of about 10 or 12 years of age. As the piece proceeds, it is the child who becomes the instructor to the teacher. You may find it useful to use a chair, steps, or other props to have the child physically "above" the teacher to express the change in roles that takes place.

READER 1   Okay, what is it?

READER 2   Why did the man want to have Jesus come to Capernaum?

READER 1   He wanted to see Jesus heal his son. But Jesus didn't need to go. Then and there Jesus healed the man's son from a distance.

READER 2   You mean Jesus didn't have to leave from where he was?

READER 1   Right!

READER 2   Then why did he have to leave heaven in the first place to have another hometown in Galilee? [*takes a step higher*]

READER 1   So we could see him and know what God was like.

READER 2   But I thought Jesus didn't want people to believe just because of what they saw?

READER 1   Right.

READER 2   So Jesus should have stayed home, so we could not see him, so we could believe in him better, right?

READER 1   Well…let me go on. Jesus told the man that his son was going to be okay. The official believed him and started going home. On the way home…

READER 2   He met his slaves who told the man his child was alive.

READER 1   Right, and he asked them the hour when he began to recover, and they said to him, "Yesterday at one in the afternoon the fever left him."

READER 2   The father realized that this was the hour when Jesus had said to him, "Your son will live." So he himself believed, along with his whole household.

READER 1   So it seems you can understand that?

READER 2   Yeah, it all depends on where Jesus lives. It's all about Jesus' home. It's about why you don't have to see what he does. [*eye to eye with the reader*]

READER 1   I don't understand you.

READER 2   You can ask questions too. [*At this point, reader 2 is higher, so that reader 1 has to look up to him/her.*]

READER 1   So, tell me, where does Jesus live?

READER 2   In the official's heart, that's the new hometown.

READER 1   Finding a home in the life of a government official was the second sign that Jesus did after coming from Judea to Galilee.

READER 2   Now you understand.

—C.M.

6. Pooling Your Efforts

John 5:1-18

This piece explores counting the cost of change and of discipleship. It also explores why we are afraid of real change and the reality that we can never go back. The cripple in the story wants to be healed about as much as he doesn't want it. Healing would mean changing and leaving a lifestyle and self-image to which he has grown accustomed. Miserable as his life is, he knows where and how he fits in.

CRIPPLE   [*talking to himself*] Great ambition I've got! Thirty-eight years at this pool and I am 20 paces closer to the water than when I started. Twenty paces in 38 years. A snail with palsy could do better! Still, it is a shady spot and one of the prime locations. I have my favorite mat given to me by Artemus the day he was healed and left. And there's the pillow Rebecca left behind the day she got healed. There's Peter's water jug and Ethniel's lamp. I do have a storehouse of possessions from others who made it to the pool before I did.

JESUS   Hello.

CRIPPLE   Oh, hello, my name's Joseph.

JESUS   Well, what a coincidence, my stepfather's name was Joseph.

CRIPPLE   Glad to meet you. You aren't lame or blind or deaf or sick like the rest of us. Are you here visiting someone? Perhaps I can help. I know everyone here. I've been here 38 years trying to be healed, so I know this place pretty well. You might say it's my home.

JESUS   I know all that. I've come to help you. Do you want to be made well?

CRIPPLE   Now that's an interesting question. I mean I am well enough off here with friends and with possessions.

JESUS   Do you want to be made well?

CRIPPLE   Well, sure I do, but it's long way to the pool, that's why I have this shady spot. You have to wait until the pool waters are stirred by the spirits and then you have to be the first in—but it's far for someone like me and there is no one to put me in the pool.

JESUS   Do you want to be made well?

CRIPPLE   Okay, so I don't have a lot of ambition to be here 38 years and to be claiming a spot only 20 paces from where I began. But I wouldn't be here day after day if I didn't want to be healed.

Production Notes

Participants:
Crippled person, Jesus

The cripple and Jesus should not introduce themselves to the audience. Let the skit unfold as written, and people will figure it out. Play it as an actual conversation. The cripple is cynical and a bit manic, going from dreaming to defensiveness in a twinkling. Note that the cripple can be played by a woman or a man.

TABOR COLLEGE LIBRARY
Hillsboro, Kansas 67063

JESUS   I can heal you.

CRIPPLE   Wouldn't that be nice if you could. Perhaps, if the water gets stirred up, you could help me beat the rush to the pool.

JESUS   Why are you afraid?

CRIPPLE   Me? Afraid? Not really. [*pause*] Well, it would mean leaving this shady spot and all my possessions and all my friends and how would I get along in the world out there? This ain't heaven, but I belong.

JESUS   Stand up, pick up your mat and walk.

CRIPPLE   Yes. Well. Thanks for the encouragement.

JESUS   Don't be afraid. Try it.

CRIPPLE   Well as you can see... My legs, I can move them. I can stand. I can...stagger like a baby on a roller coaster. Whoa. My legs are wobbly, let me sit down.

JESUS   Soon you'll get the hang of walking. It will give you a whole new perspective. Now you may go.

CRIPPLE   And do what? After 38 years I have no marketable skills, I have never held a job, no one knows me except as a CRIPPLE. What will people say? How will they react? I don't know what to do. At least as a CRIPPLE I could be a beggar.

JESUS   You are a new person. Your sins are forgiven. Do not think about the old way of being; rather, focus on new doors that can open for you. You are not alone. From this moment forward you will go with God.

CRIPPLE   Hey, don't go! Who are you? Great! I'm here alone with two good legs for the first time in my life and not an inkling about where to go or what to do. The sun is so bright outside and there are so many places I could go. Why do I still wish to go back to my spot by the pool?

—K.H.

7. It's No Mistake

John 6:1-15

In the Gospels, whenever Jesus and food are in the same story, there's often some allusion to the Lord's Supper. One does not have to read the Lord's Supper into every food event, but in this one it is apparent. It is upon the grace [the essence] of Jesus that the people feed. While the crucifixion alluded to by the Lord's Supper is not here, the process of Jesus taking, blessing, and distributing bread is. This story may be used to further the ideas in Your Life Is Ajar [page 33].

Production Notes

Participants:
Philip and Andrew

These two disciples are trying to understand what Jesus did when he fed 5000 people. A large wicker basket, under the arm, or on the floor, would be good.

PHILIP   Andrew, I'm glad you asked me to meet you at the local watering hole.

ANDREW   What I actually meant was the inn, but I guess this will do. [*reaching for a dipper and bending into a well, extending a ladle*] Care for a drink, Philip?

PHILIP   [*politely waving off the offer*] Ah, no thanks. I've been meaning to ask you about Jesus. He's not making sense lately. Know what I mean?

ANDREW   Try defining "lately." You mean, like since we met him.

PHILIP   When I first met him I thought, "Eureka! Here he is, the one with all the answers, the one who was going to lead us and free us." But, it's not like he's been loafing around. Jesus is a surprise a minute. But Andrew, tell me, what's got you so flummoxed?

ANDREW   It was the bread. Feeding 5000 was quite a surprise; that little boy was beside himself...

PHILIP   He was beside me too...

ANDREW   No, I mean even the child saw the miracle, everyone saw it. But Jesus made a mistake.

PHILIP   Wait. He picks up two loaves and five fishes and feeds 5000 people. That's about as easy as walking on water! It's like other miracles he's done.

ANDREW   Yeah, yeah, but he made a mistake. He did. I saw it and so did everyone else, even you. He took the bread, he gave thanks, he broke it, and passed it around for everyone to eat. And everyone had enough.

PHILIP   So what can be wrong with that?

ANDREW   He had us pick up the leftovers.

PHILIP   What? You think you're too good to be a holy bus boy? You're more of the maitre d' type. I saw you rounding up people like a traffic cop in Times Square when Jesus told us to have them sit in groups.

ANDREW   No it wasn't the process. It's the leftover...

PHILIP   [interrupting] What, you think he should have left them for the sparrows? Didn't you hear him say something about God knowing how many hairs were on the head of the sparrows of the field named Lilly? Or something like that. The sparrows don't need us, they've got God.

ANDREW   [exasperated] It wasn't that. It was the fact that we gathered 12 baskets of food.

PHILIP   [beginning to sound a bit resentful of Andrew] What! Now you're upset that Jesus did the miracle to feed everyone but wasn't quite exact enough to do it without leaving leftovers. That he's wasteful with God's grace, somehow just overdoing it? Is that it? Huh?

ANDREW: [Reaching into his basket, he pulls out a hunk of bread and puts it to the face of Philip.] It's this! People are dying for bread. And they'll keep coming for bread and more bread. He could have given the hungry people the bread to take home. He could have given them blessed pieces that would never run out. But no! He has us take the bread away from the people. What are they going to do when they get hungry again? They're on their own now. What kind of favor is that?

PHILIP   It's not a mistake. People will always go chasing for bread. It's not bread that will fill us.

ANDREW   You mean that, "I-am-the-bread-of-life" thing he said? What does he want us to do? Eat him up? We're not cannibals, are we? He'd have to die [pause]—for us—to eat...[He looks at the hunk of bread in his hand, and does not finish the sentence. He looks as if he is about to cry with sorrow and gratitude.]

PHILIP   [Philip puts a hand to Andrew's shoulder as if to support him. Andrew is overwhelmed with the realization. Philip speaks consolingly.] I think that's where we are headed.

ANDREW   [With awe and fear of the newly realized plan, he now speaks in a stage whisper.] So, it's not a mistake. It's a sacrifice. It's a miracle.

—C.M.

40.

8. Bread of Life

John 6:35-71

This piece tries to portray the fickleness of the disciples in their devotion and loyalty to Jesus, while portraying a constancy of love and commitment from Jesus. This reflects at least some points of the journey of many contemporary Christians.

LEADER 1	I am the bread of life.
PEOPLE	Give us this bread always.
LEADER 1	Whoever comes to me will never be hungry.
PEOPLE	Give us this bread; we are hungry.
LEADER 2	And whoever believes in me will never be thirsty.
PEOPLE	Give us this water; we are thirsty.
LEADER 2	Everything that God gives me will come to me and anyone who comes to me I will not drive away; for I have come down from heaven, not to do my will, but the will of God who sent me.
PEOPLE	We will come to you. God's will be done.
LEADER 1	And this is the will of God, that all who see the Son and believe in him may have eternal life; and I will raise them up on the last day.
PEOPLE	Wait a minute. Isn't this Jesus, son of Joseph and Mary? How can he say he has come down from heaven?
LEADER 2	Believe me. I am the bread of life. Your ancestors ate manna and died, but I am the bread from heaven. If you eat of this bread you will not die.
PEOPLE	[*disgusted*] Shall we eat flesh?
LEADER 1	I am the bread of life.
PEOPLE	This is a hard teaching and we must think about it. How can we understand it?
LEADER 2	It is not for your understanding.
PEOPLE	How can we comprehend it?
LEADER 1	It is not for your comprehension.
PEOPLE	How can we believe if we have to do this awful thing?
LEADER 2	I am not talking of flesh. It is the spirit that gives life. Listen to my teaching about spirit and life. Don't dwell on the wrong things or else you cannot believe. That is why those who come to me can only do so with God's help.
PEOPLE	Some will leave because of this teaching.
LEADER 1	Do you wish to go also?
PEOPLE	To whom would we go? Let our weak faith find strength in you. Let our lost selves be found in you. Let our yearnings to return to God be fulfilled in you.
1&2	I chose you. Now, come!!

—K.H.

Production Notes

Participants:
Two leaders, and the People.

This may be done antiphonally with Leader 1 on one side of the congregation and Leader 2 on the other. The People may be a chorus located on stage, or dispersed throughout the congregation. Or it could be grouped in another location in the meeting space. It is best when everyone puts some expression into it, avoiding the liturgical monotone "blahs." Have at least a minute of silence after the last line. Let people ponder. Say the last line with as much tenderness as you can muster.

9. Incognito

John 7:1-14, 14-24

As Jesus' popularity grows, and as suspicions about him also increase, he takes time to be alone while the disciples go on ahead to the festival. But as the story unfolds, the Jewish authorities realize they are being exposed and do not like it. So the hiding trades places. Jesus can remain incognito only so long. As Jesus reveals himself, he also uncovers us. We either accept ourselves as Jesus accepts us, or we seek to hide from him.

Production Notes

Participants:

Two readers

The piece begins with Reader 1 wearing a "Groucho Marx" disguise (black glasses, plastic nose, and fuzzy mustache). As the piece proceeds, the two readers will exchange the disguise. The pace is slow and deliberate. Allow the words to be articulated in such a way that different meanings can be heard. For instance, the word "incognito" at the beginning can be read as an accusation, a question, a statement, even a compliment. At the beginning, the two readers stand side by side, yet only vaguely aware of each other. As the reading proceeds and it gets to the point of handing off the disguise, they become aware of each other and their lines almost become a conversation.

READER 1 Incognito
Incognito
Incognito
Fuzzy eyebrows
[*takes the disguise in his hands, looks at it, puts it back on*]
Plastic nose [*points to it, or removes it briefly*]
Black glasses [*takes them off, then puts them on*]
Incognito
There he goes [*pointing to someone moving along in the distance*]

READER 2 Attracting attention
Hiding behind
Shaking disciples
Death threats
Then, out in the open
Out in the open

READER 1 Incognito
Fuzzy eyebrows
Plastic nose
Dark glasses
Incognito
There he goes [*pointing in the other direction*]

READER 1 I'll stay here. [*readers begin noticing each other*]
Then he goes
He hides out
Then he goes out!
Lagging behind
Taking the lead
Not raising his voice in the street
Removing walls of the temple with his speech [*remove the disguise and hold it out to the side to the other reader*]

READER 2 Incognito?

> [looks at the held out disguise as an opportunity to go into hiding]
> [Pauses to put on disguise. From this point on, Reader 2 express-
> es frustration and resistance to Jesus, while Reader 1 expresses
> admiration and hope in Jesus.]

READER 2 He is trouble…

> Deceiving

READER 1 He is a good man…

> Redeeming
>
> He is a wise man…
>
> Teaching

READER 2 He is like no man…[the two begin tro turn away from each other]

> Angering

READER 1 He is like no man…

> Astonishing

READER 2 Incognito

> Fuzzy eyebrows
>
> Plastic nose
>
> Dark glasses
>
> Incognito
>
> There he goes
>
> Don't judge by what you see
>
> But judge soundly
>
> Is not this the man whom they are trying to kill?
>
> And here he is, speaking openly, but they say nothing to him!
>
> Can it be that the authorities really know that this is the
> Messiah?

READER 1 You know me, and you know where I am from.

> I have not come on my own.
>
> But the one who sent me is true,
>
> and you… [pause]
>
> do not… [pause]
>
> know him.

READER 2 Incognito

> Incognito
>
> Incognito
>
> Who goes incognito?
>
> Who wears the plastic nose?
>
> Who wears the dark glasses?
>
> Who goes incognito?

> — C.M.

10. No Prophet from Galilee

John 7:32-36, 45-52

Production Notes

Participants:

Two readers

This is done in a conversational, informal style. Be prepared to pause on your lines if people laugh. Even if they don't, a pregnant pause will give them time to smirk. The two readers are narrators who sometimes take on the character of the one they are quoting. Whoever is speaking could show some level of frustration if the other is interrupting with silly comments. The last line comes out of the blue, but signifies a truth. Leave a pause to let it sink in.

READER 1 What are you looking for?

READER 2 [*looking through the script, on the floor, etc.*] I was supposed to tell a story about Jesus and he's gone.

READER 1 You mean your script?

READER 2 No, Jesus.

READER 1 Jesus?

READER 2 [*a little exasperated that the other doesn't understand*] Is gone, vanished, nil, out of sight, hidden, flown the coup...

READER 1 Wait a minute, how can Jesus vanish?

READER 2 That is the question the people in the story asked. And now, out of the blue, you ask it too. This is very scary.

READER 1 No, it's not. I was just asking a simple question to a rather silly opening by you.

READER 2 You think it's silly? Well, just listen. [*pause*] The Pharisees heard the crowd saying, "Will the Messiah do more signs than this man has done?" So they sent temple police to arrest Jesus. Jesus said, "I will be with you a little while longer, then I am going to him who sent me."

READER 1 [*aside to audience*] Whatever that means.

READER 2 "You will search for me," Jesus said, "but you will not find me, and where I am you cannot come."

READER 1 [*aside to audience*] Nya, nya, nya-nya nya.

READER 2 The police didn't understand what he was talking about.

READER 1 That's no surprise, I'm not all that sure myself.

READER 2 [*trying to explain*] The police were confused.

READER 1 [*to the audience*] They were flummoxed . . . [*Reader 2 gives Reader 1 a strange look*] [*to Reader 2*] What? It's a word!

READER 2 They went back to the temple empty-handed.

READER 1 Except one police who had his head in his hands.

READER 2 [*a little annoyed at Reader 1*] Must you?

READER 1 The temple bosses exclaimed, "What, no Jesus! What happened?"

READER 2 The police said, "Never has anyone spoken like that!"

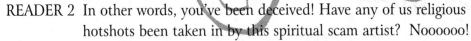

READER 1 The chief priests cried, "You've been flummoxed!" [*slight pause, smile proudly at having worked that word in again, then a side comment to the audience*] It's my word of the day.

READER 2 In other words, you've been deceived! Have any of us religious hotshots been taken in by this spiritual scam artist? Noooooo!

READER 1 But the commoners, who don't know the Law from Adam—literally—think that he's God's gift to the world!

READER 2 Nicodemus, who had spoken to Jesus before, said, "Our Law says that we shouldn't judge someone without first hearing them out."

READER 1 The others scowled at him and said, "Are you a sympathizer, now? Check the Scriptures, Nick. The words *Galilee* and *prophet* are mutually exclusive. A prophet from Galilee? That's an oxymoron. It ain't gonna happen."

READER 2 The leaders then pondered, "What did he mean that we would search but not find him? That man disappears quicker than promises after an election. Now even our police force can't locate him."

READER 1 So, there's my point. Jesus disappeared.

READER 1 Did you read the rest of the Gospel of John?

READER 2 No, just up to here. What happens in the rest of the book?

READER 1 We find out that Jesus never really disappeared. In fact, he is still among us.

READER 2 He's still . . . I don't get it. How can he still be here?

READER 1 [*touching his/her own heart*] It's an inside job.

—K.H.

11. He Said, They Said
John 7:37-44

In this sketch people simply do not agree on whether or not to trust Jesus' claims. The sides become drawn. One side seeks to deny him and even kill him. The others know him to be the gift of life.

Production Notes

Participants:
Three readers

Reader 1 and Reader 2 should stand face-to-face, while Reader 3 stands behind them looking straight out at the congregation. This would be best if memorized and shot back and forth at a rapid pace. It is an argument after all. But pause occasionally, allowing the listeners a few chances to catch up to the debate and feel the pull to choose side themselves. Another possibility is that a chorus or the congregation reads the part of Reader 2

READER 1	He said
READER 2	They said
READER 1	He said
READER 2	They said
READER 1	He said
READER 3	Let the thirsty ones come to me
READER 2	They said
READER 1	This is really a prophet
READER 2	He said
READER 3	Rivers flow from a believing heart
READER 1	They said
READER 2	This really is the Messiah
READER 1	They said
READER 2	Can't be! [*pause*]
READER 1	They said
READER 2	Messiah can't come from Galilee
READER 1	They smell like fish, have funny accents, and are
READER 2	Well, [*pause, at a loss for polite words*]… you know…
READER 1	They said
READER 2	He's the Messiah
READER 1	They said
READER 2	He's a prophet
READER 1	They said
READER 2	He's from God
READER 1	He's supposed to be from Bethlehem
READER 2	Arrest him
READER 1	He's from Galilee
READER 2	He's living water
READER 1	He's dirty water [*pause*]
READER 2	He said
READER 1	They said
READER 2	He said
READER 3	Let the thirsty ones come to me
READER 1	They said
READER 2	Arrest him [*pause*]
READER 1	He said
READER 3	Let the thirsty ones come to me
	—C.M.

12. Caught
John 8:1-11

We are all caught in life— between good and evil, between bad and worse, between joy and happiness, between things that seem equal and things that are widely different. The difference in this story is between being trapped by others and being caught by Jesus. This is about going from "between a rock and a hard place" to "putting the Rock in a heart place."

Caught. In many ways that one word could describe my whole life. Caught. As a child my family was caught in a web of poverty. We lived with my uncle, who was not rich, but he owned a house. My father was caught between the menial jobs he worked and the crushing debts he owed. My mother was caught between trying to earn extra money and the fact that women don't count for much. I first felt caught at age eight, when my uncle began taking a special interest in me. There was no one I could turn to. He was, after all, providing my family with shelter.

At 16 I did the unthinkable. I ran away and came to Jerusalem. I hoped to escape the horror of those eight years. When I left, my parents were as caught as ever in their poverty.

Then I became caught again, as a young woman without means. I met Abniel. He was kind and willing to keep me as his mistress. He was a moderately well-to-do trader. His wife was not the easiest person to get along with. The arrangement helped me to live. It was not the best arrangement, but I had no other options. I was a woman. I was caught.

Then came the day when the temple police caught me and bound me and dragged me before the temple priests. There I was accused as an adulteress and sentenced to be stoned. This time I felt I had been caught for the last time. There was no way out.

Then they brought me to him. It seemed like they wanted to catch him too. They used me as an example to try to trap him. They called him Teacher, with a mocking tone. "This woman was caught in the act of adultery. The law of Moses says we should stone her to death. What do you say, Teacher?"

He looked at them long and hard, not as one who was caught, but as one who looks on delinquent children doing mischief. I shivered to look at him

Production Notes
Participant:
A single presenter--a woman

This is a monologue that might be best done as a memorized piece, but will also be effective if read. A slight emphasis each time the word "caught" is used will serve as the drumbeat of this piece. Incorporate some movement to add interest, and use a prop or two if needed. Keep such additions sparse.

glaring at the priests. Then he knelt down and made scribbles in the dust with his finger. I thought at first he was writing something to show them. But then it seemed as though he were trying to calm a storm rising within him. It was so quiet, you could almost hear his heartbeat.

Then he said, "Let anyone of you who is without sin, cast the first stone." I closed my eyes and prayed that the first stone would knock me mercifully unconscious. Then I heard a stone drop, then another and then the sound of feet on gravel. I opened my eyes and we were alone, the Teacher and I. He came to me and, with a look that went to my very soul, he asked, "Woman, where are they? Has no one condemned you?" Bewildered, I answered, "No one, sir." He said, "Neither do I condemn you. Go your way and do not sin again from now on."

But I could not move. Even when he left, I stood there, remembering how he talked to me, the look he gave me. I was caught once again, but this was not like the other times. I was caught up in a love that washed my soul, that gave me hope. I was caught in the moment that someone had treated me like a human being.

Since then I have been forever caught...in God's loving arms.

—K.H.

13. Now I Can See

John 9

John's Gospel is rich in its use of the metaphor of light. In this piece, that theme is played out visibly, as a man born blind receives the gifts of sight and light. In reacting to the miracle, however, the Pharisees proclaim their preference for the darkness. Recalling God's words at the calling of Isaiah (Isa. 6:9-10), the blind see and seeing become blind.

PART I

NARRATOR	As he walked along, he saw a man blind from birth. His disciples asked him, "Rabbi, who sinned, this man or his parents, that he was born blind?" Jesus answered,
JESUS	Neither this man nor his parents sinned; he was born blind so that God's works might be revealed in him. We must work the works of him who sent me while it is day; night is coming when no one can work. As long as I am in the world, I am the light of the world.
NARRATOR	When he had said this, he spat on the ground and made mud with his spit. He spread the mud on the man's eyes, saying to him,
CROWDS	He did what with what? Ooo, yuck!
JESUS	Go, wash in the pool of Siloam
NARRATOR	The man went and washed and came back, able to see. The neighbors and those who had seen him before as a beggar began to ask,
CROWDS	Is this not the man who used to sit and beg?
NARRATOR	Some were saying, "It is he." Others were saying, "No, but it is someone like him." He kept saying,
BLIND MAN	I am the man.
NARRATOR	But they kept asking him,
CROWDS	How many fingers am I holding up?
NARRATOR	No! They asked him…
CROWDS	Then how were your eyes opened?
BLIND MAN	The man called Jesus made mud, spread it on my eyes, and said to me, "Go to Siloam and wash." Then I went and washed and received my sight.
CROWDS	Where is he?

Production Notes

Participants:

Narrator, Jesus, Crowds, Blind Man, Pharisees

This is a long story in three parts. It can be separated by acts of worship such as singing, sermons, offering or whatever seems appropriate to your setting. Or, it can be done as a single story. Finding different locations within the venue would help the worshipers keep track of who is speaking. Use your imagination for costumes. The Pharisees, for example, could wear mortarboards, and the blind man sunglasses.

BLIND MAN	How could I know? The last time I saw him I couldn't see yet. I mean I couldn't see last time he was around.
NARRATOR	So they dragged the formerly blind man to the Pharisees. Bad luck for him—he gets his sight back AND he's the one in trouble. It's like, "Honey, I'm home, had a great day at work, even got a raise!" Then his wife says, "Oh yeah, just for that I'm calling the cops." Anyway, where were we...? Now it was a Sabbath day when Jesus made the mud and opened his eyes. Then the Pharisees also began to ask him how he had received his sight. He said to them,
BLIND MAN	He put spit and dirt on my eyes. Then I washed, and now I see.
NARRATOR	The religious police mustn't have liked the spit part because the Pharisees, announced,
PHARISEES	This man is not from God. Surely a man from God would never put spittle-mud in someone's eye!
CROWDS	Then Jesus said, "There's mud in your eye."
NARRATOR	Actually, they didn't think he was from God because he did not observe the Sabbath. But others said,
CROWDS	"How can a man who is a sinner perform such signs?" And they were divided.
NARRATOR	So everyone in the whole town said
CROWDS	Hmmmm? Hmmm?
NARRATOR	In order to keep feathers ruffled, some expressed the opinion that the man formerly known as the man blind from birth, was not actually blind from birth. An investigative team from the local eyewitness news team tracked down his parents for a comment. Had their son, or had not their son, the man formerly know as the man blind since birth, actually been blind since birth? "Just the facts, ma'am."
CROWDS	"Yes," was their reply. "Otherwise all that bumping into things and tripping over the dog was all just a hoax. Surely he wasn't faking all these years. If you don't mind, we'd like get home now. We think we might need to finally paint our son's room now that he might actually care about color."
NARRATOR	His parents said this because they were afraid of the Jews; for the Jews had already agreed that anyone who confessed Jesus to be the Messiah would be put out of the synagogue.

PART II

NARRATOR	For the second time they called the man who had been blind, and they said to him,
PHARISEES	Give credit to God, for your sight. We know that Jesus is a sinner.
BLIND MAN	I don't know who he was, and he didn't seem like much of a sinner to me. What I do know is that I was blind, and now I see.
PHARISEES	But what did he do to you? How did he restore your sight?
CROWDS	You're so wound up about this, you must want to follow him too.
PHARISEES	[*make a bunch of growly noises, like they are about to swear up a storm*]
NARRATOR	[*clears throat to restore order*] They reviled the man, the man formerly known as the man born blind. Suddenly it became clear to the man formerly known as the man born blind, that when one is physically blind, other senses compensate to create understanding. When people are spiritually blind, there is nothing else to compensate—they're just stupid.
CROWDS	Here's the astonishing thing the formerly blind man said:
BLIND MAN	You don't know where he comes from, nor where he goes. But so what! He opened my eyes. If this man were not from God, he could do nothing. But he does do something!
NARRATOR	The Pharisees got mad at the man and drove him out, saying,
PHARISEES	You were born in sin and have been a sinner ever since, and you dare to teach us?!

PART III

NARRATOR	But Jesus heard about the man's predicament—how his parents did not protect him, how the crowds just stared in dumb amazement, and how the Pharisees had mistreated, abused, and reviled him. Finally after the inquisitors had taken their shot at the man formerly known as the man born blind, Jesus came up to him, and asked,
JESUS	Do you believe in the Son of Man?
BLIND MAN	And who is he, sir?
JESUS	You have seen him, and the one speaking with you is he.

CROWDS   Lord, I believe.

NARRATOR   He believed and he saw. Believing is seeing. Someone
              receives sight and believes, while others grow blind in their
              unbelief.

JESUS   I came into this world for judgment so that those who do
              not see may see, and those who do see may become blind.

NARRATOR   Jesus said this within earshot of the-not-yet-deaf-also-
              Pharisees. Of course, they had to ask,

PHARISEES   Surely we are not blind, are we? Wouldn't someone know if
              they're blind or not?

NARRATOR   So, with a twinkle and a tear in his eyes, Jesus had to tell
              them,

JESUS   If you were blind, you would not have sin. But now that you
              say, "We see," your sin remains.

NARRATOR   Jesus: One who gives sight to the blind, banishing all blind-
              ness. Jesus: One who blinds those overcome by misguided
              pride, leaving them to their chosen darkness.

              —C.M.

14. Dead to the World
John 11:1-50

This loose rendition of the story of Lazarus has some humorous threads, including the inability of people to understand what Jesus was really saying.

READER 2 Now, a certain man named Lazarus was ill...

READER 3 [*impishly*] DEATHLY ill!

READER 2 [*to 3*] You're going to spoil the story.

READER 3 [*ignoring 2*] Anyway. Mary, the one who anointed Jesus with cologne...

READER 2 PERFUME!

READER 3 Whatever... and dried his feet with her hair...

READER 2 Now there's an image.

READER 3 This same woman and her sister Martha were siblings to Lazarus and friends of Jesus.

READER 2 The sisters sent a message to Jesus, saying "He whom you love is ill."

READER 1 Jesus, [*an aside to the audience*] that's me, said "Let's stick around this place for a few days longer; it's not like Lazarus is going to die or something.

READER 3 [*to Jesus*] Lazarus died.

READER 1 Oh. Bit of a bad call on my part, do you think?

READER 3 Maybe medicine is not your field.

READER 1 Don't worry, things will work out for God's glory. Let's go to Judea, you disciples. [*motions to 4&5*]

READER 4 Rabbi, the church leaders there threw stones at you and yelled bad names.

READER 5 Yeah, let's at least wait until they mature enough to TALK out their differences.

READER 1 Look, [*counts on his fingers*] (a) there are 12 hours in a day; (b) those who walk in the day don't stumble because they see the light; and (c) those who walk at night stumble because they do not have the light in them.
[*pause*]

READER 4 I'm with that last group.

READER 5 Yeah, me too.

READER 1 [*tries again to explain*] Lazarus is sleeping and I am going to wake him up.

READER 5 Is that a good idea?

Production Notes
Participants:
Reader 1 as Jesus; Reader 2 as a narrator and Martha; Reader 3 as a narrator and Lazarus; Readers 4 and 5 as Disciples and Pharisees

Note the dual roles of all the readers except Jesus, and practice their transitions. Be conscious of pacing and pause for laughter.

READER 4 If he was sick, he'll need his rest.

READER 1 [*exasperated*] Lazarus is DEAD! I was using a metaphor!. Here comes Martha. Try to pay attention.

READER 2 Jesus, Lazarus has been dead for four days. I wish pagers had been invented, then we could have gotten you to come sooner.

READER 1 Your brother will rise again.

READER 2 Oh sure, on the last day, like everyone else.

READER 1 I am the resurrection and the life. Those who believe in me, even though they die, will live, and everyone who lives and believes in me will never die. Do you believe this?

READER 2 Yes, I believe that you are the Messiah.

READER 4 [*to 5*] Did you get all that?

READER 5 I'm still working on the day and night thing a couple of pages back.

READER 1 Where is Lazarus laid?

READER 3 Come and see.

READER 1 Take away the stone.

READER 2 Is that necessary? The smell would knock a buzzard off a garbage heap.

READER 1 Didn't I say you'd see God's glory? Now, God, I pray to you so that everyone around may hear me. I know that you are always listening to me. Do this so that they might believe that you sent me. Lazarus, come out.

READER 2 And Lazarus came out of the tomb and said...

READER 3 Mmph, mmph, mmph!

READER 1 Unbind him and let him go!

READER 3 Many believed in Jesus because of what he did.

READER 2 But others went to the Pharisees and told them.

READER 3 And the Pharisees said...

READER 4 We can't let him bring people back from the dead. He must be stopped.

READER 5 Let's kill Jesus before he starts another religion and the Romans come and destroy us all.

READER 4 Yes, let's kill him before the whole nation is destroyed. You never know where this Christ worship will lead.

READER 2 And so Jesus hid himself for a time.

READER 3 Until the time was ready for him to go to Jerusalem one last time.

—K.H

15. Lazarus's Soliloquy
John 12:9-10

Lazarus has just been through an uplifting, miraculous experience: resurrection from the dead. The Pharisees, however, are so against Jesus and anything that heightens his popularity that now Lazarus becomes a target.

To be or not to be, that is the question.
I have been and [*thoughtfully*] not been, then been again. [*confused*]
It is said that, "It is appointed that a man die once,"
Well what about me? [*pause*]
Now they want to un-do me.
Life isn't fair, death isn't fair, and neither is a second life.
I believe that death is there as that final battle,
A place for weeding out the unnecessary, the flotsam and jetsam of life
The drift wood
Washed up, bleached out, burned up.
To be or to be un-be-ed, that is ah… um…, yeah, the question.
Now that I am be-ing again, the Pharisees want to un-be me.
[*reflective pause, then, with conviction*] Life is good!
From the depths of a tomb
I heard my name.
My soul groggily stirred as if from deep sleep.
My name… [*reminiscing*] I heard…
The voice of a friend.
To be or not to be?
By the voice of God I was formed
In my mother's womb,
By the voice of God,
I rose from a tomb.
By the voice of God I will be drawn onward
And rise to heaven.

—C.M.

Production Notes

Participant:
Single presenter, preferably a man

As a monologue, this works best if memorized. There is a play on words from Shakespeare's Hamlet ("To be or not to be…") that needs to spoken clearly, due to the use of non-words like "un-be." Speak them clearly but don't overemphasize them to the extent that they become out of balance with the rest of the piece. Note that the ending has Lazarus expressing a "come what may" kind of confidence, as if no one can kill his spirit, which hears God's voice all the time now.

16. The Hour Has Come

John 12:23b-50

It is the beginning of the end for Jesus. As he offers the crowds an opportunity to respond to God, however, they still do not understand who he is, or what he has come to do.

Production Notes

Participants: *Leader, chorus*

This piece is taken straight from the Bible (NRSV), illustrating what can be done with dramatic presentations of Scripture. The choral parts are short so as to keep the performance sounding tight. Though short, be sure not to rush the reading, nor to read it in an unnatural rhythm.

LEADER Jesus answered them, "The hour has come for the Son of Man to be glorified. Very truly, I tell you, unless a grain of wheat falls into the earth and dies, it remains just a single grain; but if it dies, it bears much fruit. Those who love their life lose it, and those who hate their life in this world will keep it for eternal life. Whoever serves me must follow me, and where I am, there will my servant be also. Whoever serves me, the Father will honor.

CHORUS "Now my soul is troubled. And what should I say...

LEADER 'Father, save me from this hour'? No, it is for this reason that I have come to this hour. Father, glorify your name.'" Then a voice came from heaven, "I have glorified it, and I will glorify it again." The crowd standing there heard it and said that it was thunder. Others said, "An angel has spoken to him." Jesus answered, "This voice has come for your sake, not for mine. Now is the judgment of this world; now the ruler of this world will be driven out. And I, when I am lifted up from the earth, will draw all people to myself." He said this to indicate the kind of death he was to die. The crowd answered him, "We have heard from the law that the Messiah remains forever. How can you say that the Son of Man must be lifted up? Who is this Son of Man?" Jesus said to them,

CHORUS "The light is with you for a little longer.

LEADER "Walk while you have the light, so that the darkness may not overtake you. If you walk in the darkness, you do not know where you are going. While you have the light, believe in the light, so that you may become children of light." After Jesus had said this, he departed and hid from them. Although he had performed so many signs in their presence, they did not believe in him. This was to fulfill the word spoken by the prophet Isaiah: "Lord, who has believed our message, and to whom has the arm of the Lord been revealed?" And so they could not believe, because Isaiah also said, "He has blinded their eyes and hardened their heart, so that they might not look with their eyes, and understand with their heart and turn— and I would heal them." Isaiah said this because he saw his glory and spoke about him. Nevertheless many, even of the authorities, believed in him. But because of the Pharisees they did not confess it, for fear that they would be put out of the synagogue; for they loved human glory more than the glory that comes from God.

CHORUS Then Jesus cried aloud:

LEADER "Whoever believes in me believes not in me but in him who sent me. And whoever sees me sees him who sent me. I have come as light into the world, so that everyone who believes in me should not remain in the darkness. I do not judge anyone who hears my words and does not keep them, for I came not to judge the world, but to save the world. The one who rejects me and does not receive my word has a judge; on the last day the word that I have spoken will serve as judge, for I have not spoken on my own, but the Father who sent me has himself given me a commandment about what to say and what to speak. And I know that his commandment is eternal life.

CHORUS "What I speak, therefore, I speak...

LEADER "...just as the Father has told me... just as the Father has told me."

—C.M.

17. Wash Me
John 13:1-35

What kind of conviction did Judas have in carrying out his task of betraying Jesus? Here is one scenario that shows him as savvy, one of the few disciples who has an inkling of what Jesus' real agenda is. This portrait may be viewed by some as too gentle on such a soul as Judas. But it also may draw out his similarities to us, which may be what scares us about him. If he was as perceptive as he is portrayed here, it makes his action all the more tragic.

Production Notes

Participant:

Judas

This is a monologue done in a "dark" tone. Judas is reflecting on what just happened in the upper room. He has just departed and is standing outside the room in the hallway, on his way to the temple priests to help them arrest Jesus. Dim lighting and dark clothing would help the atmosphere. A spotlight on Judas could accent his solitude. Resist the temptation to tell people who you are, either in the monologue or in the title.

I sit here by the door, alone in the hallway, listening to the murmur of voices in the room. I cannot leave, but I must. I cannot reenter but I want to.

Jesus has said some disturbing things tonight. I am beginning to understand some of what he has tried to do these past few years.

It is Passover night, and I had been hoping for a traditional Seder meal. I anticipated a quiet evening. By now I should have known that that kind of evening rarely works out for us.

Jesus was in one of his teaching modes and had a melancholy air about him, like a shroud. As he talked his eyes moved about the room with a faraway look. I think he was assessing what he knew to be his last meal with us all. It had been three long, hard, wonderful, confusing, and adventurous years.

His mood at supper affected us, because we all talked in hushed tones. The conversation seemed to move around Jesus. He was unreachable, untouchable.

After supper, he suddenly arose and took off his robe. We watched as he tied a towel around his waist and took a basin of water. He began to wash our feet. Ironically, the first to have his washed was me. I never looked him in the eye. He never said a word.

Then he had an awkward encounter with Peter. Peter objected to having Jesus wash his feet. He didn't get it. When Jesus rebuked him, then Peter wanted a bath! What a bumbler! I don't know what Jesus sees in that man. Over the years I have marveled that such a large head seems to house such a small brain—yet Jesus was always patient with people like him. Jesus loved all of us the whole time we were with him. Even when he chastised us, we felt his love. [*reflective pause*]

I shuddered when he commented, "Not all of you are clean." That sent a chill down my spine! It was like a final judgement. Like a door closing, leaving me forever on the other side. Then he explained why he washed our feet. He wanted us to serve one another in the same way, and be servants in the world. I'm not sure everyone in the room got it, but it was clear to me. In his unique way, Jesus had struck to the heart of the matter with that simple act.

Then he added, "The one who ate my bread has lifted his heel against me." I must have flushed, because I felt my face go hot. I felt dizzy. If he knew something, why didn't he just come out and say it?

Then I felt completely nailed when he finally said, "One of you will betray me." We all stared like sheep facing a lion. Everyone wondered who Jesus was talking about. [*slowly, dramatically*] "It is the one to whom I give this piece of bread when I have dipped it in the dish," he said in a low voice, so that few if any heard him. Then he dipped the bread and gave it to me! It was all I could do to hold my hand steady to take it.

He knew I would betray him and now I knew I would go through with it. "Go quickly and do what you must," he told me, [*anguished*] with those same sad, piercing, loving eyes. I left quickly, expecting the others to move against me, but no one budged. I remember their perplexed faces. They did not understand what had just happened.

So here I am, outside the door. I stopped as soon as the door closed behind me—closed forever. I will forever be on the outside. I feel some relief that my action seems chosen for me. But even more, I dread what it all means...the incredible loss! [*begins to weep, shaking*]

I can't help it...these tears begin to flow...washing me. I remember another washing, just a little while ago, a washing that brought relief and peace and warmth and acceptance. But now I leave, to carry out my obligation. And there, on the other side of the door, I hear Jesus giving his farewell speech. What's he saying? I hear it: "By this everyone will know that you are my disciples, if you have love for one another."

Will I ever feel clean again?

—K.H.

18. I've Got a Better Idea
John 13:36-38

Peter's inclination to deny Jesus begins to emerge in this retelling of the exchange between them in the upper room. Peter recognizes that Jesus' words force one to difficult conclusions; he would rather soften those words by interpreting them symbolically or leaving them in the spiritual realm. The hard sayings of Jesus still haunt us today.

Production Notes

Participants:

Peter, Jesus

Peter walks around, thinking, scheming, and looking for a better marketing plan. Jesus remains firm, speaking slowly and evenly. Jesus portrays steadfastness, and Peter's pacing back and forth testify to his attempt to avoid the straight truths Jesus is voicing.

JESUS   I give you a new commandment, that you love one another.

PETER   That's such a harsh term. Make *suggestions*, Lord, not "commandments." And "new" is out, *old fashioned* is in. But love, that's a good idea; let's stick with it.

JESUS   Just as I have loved you, you also should love one another.

PETER   Now, Lord [*said in a condescending manner*], we need some clarification. [*a little whiny*] We're all different, Lord, we're individuals with our own ways of doing things. This "one another" thing is too general.

JESUS   By this everyone will know that you are my disciples, if you have love for one another.

PETER   Well, it's true that we are yours but we've all got that god within us. We might think about rephrasing that *disciple* thing too; it sounds so, so, well, you know—like discipline. Call us your "little sunbeams" or something. I guess that *love* thing would be a good selling point. At least you're not telling us to turn water into wine, walk on water, or multiply bread.

[*pause*]

PETER   Lord, where are you going? Are you going where you said you'd be going? Are you going where I think your going? Are you going to take me with you?

JESUS.   Where I am going, you cannot follow me now; but you will follow afterward.

PETER.   Lord, why can I not follow you now? What if I want to follow you now! Can you force me not to follow you now What if I follow you now anyway?

JESUS.   I will lay down my life for you.

PETER   [*surprised and disappointed*] Oh. [*a bit indignant*] Oh. [*even more indignant*] Oh.

JESUS   Will you lay down your life for me?

PETER   Ah, well, I think that... Is that my wife calling? It must be supper time.

JESUS   We just ate.

PETER   Ah, well I... think...it will take awhile for my retirement plan to
        mature.

JESUS   Will you lay down your life for me?

PETER   Jesus, I kinda had my eye on a new fishing boat, or one of those
        new SUVs with six ox-power. It really moves.

JESUS   Will you lay down your life for me? Will you?

PETER   This is what it all comes down to, isn't it?

JESUS   Will you lay down your life...for me?

PETER   [rhetorically and sarcastically, possibly with a slight chuckle] Will I
        lay down my life for you? [then, as if catching on that Jesus is seri-
        ous] Will I lay down my life...my life, for you? [motions with his
        hands, his body language, that he wants to make some reply other
        than yes, but not wanting to say say no]
        [pause]

JESUS   Very truly, I tell you, before the cock crows, you will have denied
        me three times.
        [Both readers freeze on this last line. If possible the stage should go
        completely black on the last word.]

        —C.M.

19. Flummoxed

John 14:1-14

Often in the Gospel of John, people do not understand what Jesus was talking about. We can be pretty smug 2000 years after the fact and say we understand much better than the disciples did. Maybe so, but do we really understand Jesus' stories and teachings? If discipleship isn't the hardest thing we have ever tried to do, maybe we are doing it wrong.

Production Notes

Participants:

Three readers who begin as narrators, then assume the roles of Thomas (1), Philip (2), and Jesus (3)

This is another piece that looks at the lighter side of the disciples not "getting it." The humor is meant to both highlight what Jesus said, and add poignancy to the situation the disciples were in.

READER 1	Philip and Thomas were puzzled.
READER 2	They were downright flummoxed.
READER 3	Jesus was trying to lay things out for them.
READER 2	Like a remedial class in discipleship.
	[pause]
READER 3	"Do not let your hearts be troubled," said Jesus.
READER 2	Philip whispered to Thomas, "My heart isn't troubled, is yours?"
READER 1	Thomas whispered back: "It is now. Why would Jesus say don't worry, unless we were supposed to be worried?"
READER 2	What are we supposed to be worried about?
READER 1	I don't know! That's what I'm worried about.
READER 2	I'm worried about you.
READER 3	Jesus went on: "Believe in God, and believe in me also. In my Father's house there are many dwelling places. If it were not so, would I have told you that I go to prepare a place for you?"
READER 1	Why would we need another place?
READER 2	Probably wants us to settle down. When was the last time you slept at home?
READER 1	Good point.
READER 3	And if I go and prepare a place for you, I will come again and take you to myself, so that where I am you will be also.
READER 2	Come again?
READER 1	Now I'm really worried. He never said anything before about leaving.
READER 2	Actually, he didn't say anything about leaving this time either.
READER 1	But he said he's coming back. How can he do that if he's still here?
READER 2	Maybe he left when we weren't looking.
READER 3	And you know the way to the place I am going.
READER 1	*[turning to Reader 3]* Excuse me, Jesus, Thomas here. We actually haven't a clue where you are going. How can we know the way?

READER 3   I am the way and the truth and the life. No one comes to the Father except through me.

READER 1   [*turning to Reader 2, deflated*] I thought it was a simple question. Why does he have to give such a convoluted answer?

READER 2   Maybe he meant he could show us the way.

READER 1   Must have. How can someone BE the way?

READER 2   We can't walk through him!

READER 3   If you know me you will know my Father also. From now on you do know him and have seen him.

READER 2   Uh oh. He's ranting again. [*turns to Reader 3*] Excuse me, Jesus—Philip there. It's very nice of you to want to show us the Father, except I can't really see him. Maybe if we could actually see him, we'd be satisfied.

READER 3   Have I been with you all this time, Philip, and you still do not know me?

READER 2   Well . . .

READER 3   Whoever has seen me has seen the Father. How can you say, "Show us the Father"?

READER 2   Actually . . .

READER 3   Do you not believe that I am in the Father and the Father is in me? The words that I say to you I do not speak on my own; but the Father who dwells in me does his works. Believe me that I am in the Father and the Father is in me; then if you do not, then believe me because of the works themselves.

READER 1   [*tugs at Reader 2's arm*] Philip, don't provoke him by trying to explain what you mean.

READER 2   But I get scared when he talks like that. I want to believe in him, but . . .

READER 1   I know. I feel we are missing something, but I have trouble getting a handle on it.

READER 2   How can we ever hope to carry on his ministry if we can't even understand what he is talking about!

READER 3   Very truly I tell you, the one who believes in me will also do the works that I do and, in fact, will do greater works than these, because I am going to the Father.

READER 1   There! He's leaving. How are we supposed to get along if he goes?

READER 3   I will do whatever you ask in my name, so that the Father may be glorified in the Son. If in my name you ask me for anything, I will do it.

READER 1   My head hurts from trying to understand this stuff.

READER 2   Didn't you hear him? Seems like we will be able to get in
           touch with him when he's gone. We just send our request and
           he'll do it.

READER 1   Long distance miracles? I'm not sure about that.

READER 2   Thomas, you question everything. You'll get a reputation.

READER 1   Philip, this discipleship thing is so hard.

READER 2   I know. It's the hardest thing I've ever tried to do.

—K.H.

20. Vines
John 15:1-15

While this teaching of Jesus precedes one of the most heart-wrenching passages in John's Gospel—the Passion story—it proclaims one of the most comforting promises: that Jesus can live in us as we live in him. The offhanded, often confusing non sequiturs presented here represent the maze of mental gymnastics we may go through to get away from, or get a grip on, what Jesus is all about.

READER 1 I am the true vine, and my Father is the vine grower. He removes every branch in me that bears no fruit. Every branch that bears fruit he prunes to make it bear more fruit.

READER 2 Dried fruit.

READER 3 Not prunes, pruning.

READER 2 Dried fruit.

READER 3 Pruning.

READER 2 Cut it out already!

READER 1 You have already been cleansed by the word that I have spoken to you.

READER 2 Not cutting! Cleansing.

READER 3 You have to clean fruit before you eat it

READER 2 Abide in me as I abide in you. Just as the branch cannot bear fruit by itself unless it abides in the vine, neither can you unless you abide in me.

READER 3 You ever think about paisley?

READER 2 Huh?

READER 3 You know, the print on ties. Paisley, you know.

READER 2 Huh?

READER 3 Well I've always thought that abiding in the vine would look like wearing a lot of paisley fabrics.

READER 2 Oh.

READER 1 I am the vine, you are the branches. Those who abide in me and I in them bear much fruit, because apart from me you can do nothing.

READER 2 Nothing?

READER 3 That's right, nothing.

READER 2 I just spoke, didn't I?

READER 3 Well, you can't do much more than that. Anyway in the great scheme of things, that's still nothing.

READER 2 But it's something.

Production Notes
Participants:
Three readers

Reader 1, standing to one side, speaks the words of Jesus. Then, at a table, or in chairs facing each other, Readers 2 and 3 are in the process of trying to under-stand. They are arguing like a couple of Hasidic stu-dents, bobbing and bowing and dancing as they speak.

READER 3 Is not.

READER 2 Is too.

READER 3 Then what is it?

READER 2 Oh, not much.

READER 1 Whoever does not abide in me is thrown away like a branch and withers; such branches are gathered, thrown into the fire, and burned.

READER 2 Keep one branch out to put marshmallows onto.

READER 3 You can't roast marshmallows on that kind of fire.

READER 2 It's a real fire isn't it?

READER 1 If you abide in me, and my words abide in you, ask for whatever you wish, and it will be done for you. My Father is glorified by this, that you bear much fruit and become my disciples. As the Father has loved me, so I have loved you; abide in my love. If you keep my commandments, you will abide in my love, just as I have kept my Father's commandments and abide in his love. I have said these things to you so that my joy may be in you, and that your joy may be complete. This is my commandment, that you love one another as I have loved you. No one has greater love than this, to lay down one's life for one's friends. You are my friends if you do what I command you. I do not call you servants any longer, because the servant does not know what the master is doing; but I have called you friends, because I have made known to you everything that I have heard from my Father.

—C.M.

21. Jesus, Tell Us

John 16:7–15

Once again the Gospel dwells on the theme of understanding. In a way this piece is a continuation of Script 20, in that the final message is that a close relationship with God will provide what we need.

VOICE 1 Jesus, tell us what we must do, but tell it soft, for we cannot bear the whole truth. Stay with us, we pray.

VOICE 2 I tell you the truth: it is to your advantage that I go away, for if I do not go away the Advocate will not come to you; but if I go, I will send him to you.

VOICE 1 Jesus, do not leave us! We need you! Why must you go? Who is this Advocate? What will he do? How will he help us?

VOICE 2 And when he comes he will prove the world wrong about sin and about righteousness and about judgment: about sin, because they do not believe in me; about righteousness, because I am going to the Father and you will see me no longer; about judgment, because the ruler of this world has been condemned. I still have many things to say to you, but you cannot bear them now. When the Spirit of truth comes, he will guide you into all the truth; for he will not speak on his own, but will speak whatever he hears, and he will declare to you the things that are to come. He will glorify me, because he will take what is mine and declare it to you. All that the Father has is mine. For this reason I said he will take what is mine and declare it to you.

VOICE 1 Please don't leave us alone! Murmur words of encouragement. Whisper words of wisdom. Tell us what we should do.

VOICE 2 I still have many things to tell you, but you cannot bear them now. When the Spirit of Truth comes, then you will be guided into all truth: for he will not speak on his own, but will speak whatever he hears, and he will declare to you the things that are to come.

VOICE 1 Will we remember you? Will you remember us? We are afraid of being alone.

VOICE 2 The Spirit will glorify me, taking what is mine and declaring it to you. All that God has is mine.
[*This reading may be followed by a hymn, such as " Oyenos mi Dios" or "Obey My Voice."*]

—K.H.

Production Notes

Participants:
Two voices

This is a type of litany for congregation (Voice 1) and leader (Voice 2). It may also be performed by two individuals, or a chorus (Voice 1) and a reader (Voice 2).

22. The Outcast
John 17

Production Notes

Participants: *Chorus and Reader*

The complexity level for this piece is high, and refinement through practice is crucial. The single actor who reads the five sections of the prayer of Jesus will begin the piece at the margins of the meeting place and process toward the front, or center—whichever seems most appropriate for your setting. Following the central section of the reading, he or she will then process back toward the margins. All the while, he or she will read the text clearly, deliberately, and slowly, but at an even pace. This reading will be the "foreground" of the piece. Meanwhile, in the "background" a choral group will voice other words. For the first part of the piece, Chant 1, their words describe the marginalized and outcast of this world. Midway through the piece this chant is exchanged for the words of supplication in

As the distinction between Jesus and the world becomes more apparent, it is all the more imperative for the reader of the Gospel to decide which side of that divide to stand upon.

CHORUS: CHANT 1

abandoned; forsaken; outcast; left till last; friendless; unwanted; unasked and loveless; misunderstood; left out; thrown out; cast out; cast away; ripped away; deep-sixed; given up; uninvited; disregarded; ignored; brushed off and killed; untouchable; heretic and leper; thrown overboard; thrown away; set aside; left alone; jettisoned; tossed aside; loneliness; eliminated; passed up; ; ruled out; refused; brushed off; reject and rejected [*last time only, leading up to Pause 3, repeat three times during the pause*] They do not belong to the world, just as I do not belong to the world.

CHORUS: CHANT 2

Glorify

Sanctify

Unify

MAIN SCRIPT, BY SINGLE READER

After Jesus had spoken these words, he looked up to heaven and said: [*processing slowly toward front, or center*] Father, the hour has come; glorify your Son so that the Son may glorify you, since you have given him authority over all people, to give eternal life to all whom you have given him. And this is eternal life, that they may know you, the only true God, and Jesus Christ whom you have sent. I glorified you on earth by finishing the work that you gave me to do. So now, Father, glorify me in your own presence with the glory that I had in your presence before the world existed.

[*Pause 1. Chorus lines should be distinct, echoing in the pause.*]

I have made your name known to those whom you gave me from the world. They were yours, and you gave them to me, and they have kept your word. Now they know that everything you have given me is from you; for the words that you gave to me I have given to them, and they have received them and know in truth that I came from you; and they have believed that you sent me. I am asking on their behalf; I am not asking on behalf of the world, but on behalf of those whom you gave me, because they are yours. All mine are yours, and yours are mine; and I have been glorified in them.

[*Pause 2. Chant rises in intensity.*]

And now I am no longer in the world, but they are in the world, and I am coming to you. Holy Father, protect them in your name that you have given me, so that they may be one, as we are one. While I was with them, I protected them in your name that you have given me. I guarded them, and not one of them was lost except the one destined to be lost, so that the scripture might be fulfilled. But now I am coming to you, and I speak these things in the world so that they may have my joy made complete in themselves. I have given them your word, and the world has hated them because they do not belong to the world, just as I do not belong to the world.

[*Pause 3. Chorus chants the final line of Chant 1 three times with intensity, then switches to Chant 2*]

[*By this time, reader should be in center of audience. With gestures, show that the audience is "they" and that the reader is "I" (Jesus).*] I am not asking you to take them out of the world, but I ask you to protect them from the evil one. They do not belong to the world, just as I do not belong to the world. Sanctify them in the truth; your word is truth. As you have sent me into the world, so I have sent them into the world. And for their sakes I sanctify myself, so that they also may be sanctified in truth. I ask not only on behalf of these, but also on behalf of those who will believe in me through their word, that they may all be one. As you, Father, are in me and I am in you, may they also be in us, so that the world may believe that you have sent me.

[*Pause 4. Chant 2 subsides in volume, but remains intense.*]

The glory that you have given me I have given them, so that they may be one, as we are one, I in them and you in me, that they may become completely one, so that the world may know that you have sent me and have loved them even as you have loved me. Father, I desire that those also, whom you have given me, may be with me where I am, to see my glory, which you have given me because you loved me before the foundation of the world. Righteous Father, the world does not know you, but I know you; and these know that you have sent me. I made your name known to them, and I will make it known, so that the love with which you have loved me may be in them, and I in them.

[*Chorus whispers Chant 2 three times.*]

—C.M.

Chant 2: "glorify, sanctify, and unify." Find a semi-rap type rhythm for both chants.

Start Chant 1 very softly, slightly before the main reader begins. It is fine if the audience cannot make out the words at first. Then let the chant rise and fall in volume, and vary the intensity and tone, according to what Jesus is praying. By the time Jesus speaks of not fitting in with the world (after Pause 2), the words should be clear. Time Chant 1 so that the last line, repeated three times, coincides with Pause 3, when the chant should become quite loud and insistent. Following on its heels, the group will switch to Chant 2, beginning with greater volume, then diminishing, chanting the three words repeatedly with joy. As they do so, the main reader retraces the steps toward the margins and, if using a cordless microphone, leaving the auditorium altogether. The chorus should repeat Chant 2 three times following the reader's exit.

23. Am I Not to Drink the Cup?

John 18:1-12

This fictitious dialogue between Peter and Jesus has the tone of a parent who is focused on a serious matter and a child who is unaware of its importance. It is amazing that the disciples seem so clueless about the greater things that are unfolding around them. Perhaps our preoccupation with peripheral things prevents us too from accepting the cup and following Jesus' way.

Production Notes

Participants: *Narrator, Peter, Jesus, Soldier*

The last line rings an ominous note, because we too are asked to drink the cup that Jesus has drunk, the cup of obedience.

NARRATOR	After Jesus had spoken these words, he went out with his disciples across the Kidron Valley to the place where there was a garden, which he and his disciples entered. Now Judas, who betrayed him, also knew the place, because Jesus often met there with his disciples. So Judas brought a detachment of soldiers together with police from the chief priests and Pharisees, and they came there with lanterns and torches and weapons.
PETER	Good. No one has taken our favorite spot.
JESUS	Peter, it's past sunset, no one but us is ever in the garden after dark.
PETER	How about I cut up some firewood.
JESUS	Peter, put away that new sword before you do some damage. We have enough firewood. You don't need a sword anyway.
PETER	Hey, look, someone is coming. Whoa, looks like a lot of people, going by the lanterns and torches. Those are Roman soldiers. Hey, there's Judas. What is he doing with them?
JESUS	He is fulfilling his appointed task.
PETER	Oh, did you send him out to bring these people back?
JESUS	In a manner of speaking. [*to those approaching*] Whom are you seeking?
SOLDIER	Jesus of Nazareth.
JESUS	I am he.
PETER	Wow, good one Jesus. You knocked them all down with just three words.
JESUS	Peter, please stay behind me. [*long pause*] Well, get up all of you. Come and take the one whom you are seeking.

SOLDIER   Jesus of Nazareth.
JESUS   Yes, I am he. So take me and let these others go.
PETER   Stand back, Lord. Run, and I'll keep them occupied.
JESUS   Peter, I said to put away your sword. Now you have injured
               someone. You will deny me soon enough, but you will not
               take away this moment. Am I not to drink the cup that God
               has given me?

               —K.H.

24. Voices

John 18:13-38

At the trial of Jesus before the High Priest Annas, Peter hangs around in the court-yard. Then as we all know, he blows it. He denies three times that he knows Jesus. In this piece, however, let us treat Peter with grace, knowing we too could have done the same.

Production Notes

Participants:

Narrator, at least three voices, Peter

Three voices, scattered throughout the room, speak to Peter. If performed in a flexible space, Peter should be in the center of the room. If the room is rather static, Peter should be at the front, on stage. The stage has the advantage of elevating Peter and providing a way to hide a floor light behind something. The room is as dark as possible, with the only light on Peter. Place a candle or lantern underneath his face so as to resemble the fire's light, or a lantern on the floor hidden behind something. Not lit from above. The end comes quickly in this piece, thus forcing one to make the most of the few words afforded Peter.

NARRATOR   First they took him to Annas, the father-in-law of Caiaphas, the high priest that year. Caiaphas was the one who had advised the Jews that it was better to have one person die for the people. Simon Peter and another disciple followed Jesus. Since that disciple was known to the high priest, he went with Jesus into the courtyard of the high priest, but Peter was standing outside at the gate. So the other disciple, who was known to the high priest, went out, spoke to the woman who guarded the gate, and brought Peter in. The woman said to Peter, "You are not also one of this man's disciples, are you?"

VOICE 1   Are you one of this man's disciples? Are you?

PETER   No, I am not.

NARRATOR   He said he was not. [*pause*] Now the slaves and the police had made a charcoal fire because it was cold, and they were standing around it and warming themselves. Peter also was standing with them and warming himself. Then the high priest questioned Jesus about his disciples and about his teaching. Jesus answered, "I have spoken openly to the world; I have always taught in synagogues and in the temple, where all the Jews come together. I have said nothing in secret. Why do you ask me? Ask those who heard what I said to them; they know what I said."

When he had said this, one of the police standing nearby struck Jesus on the face, saying, "Is that how you answer the high priest?" Jesus answered, "If I have spoken wrongly, testify to the wrong. But if I have spoken rightly, why do you strike me?" Then Annas sent him bound to Caiaphas the high priest. [*pause*] Now Simon Peter was standing and warming himself. They asked him,

VOICE 2   You are not also one of his disciples, are you?

PETER   I am not.

NARRATOR   He denied it. [*pause*] One of the slaves of the high priest, a
                 relative of the man whose ear Peter had cut off, asked,

VOICE 3   Did I not see you in the garden with him?

PETER   No! No. [*then mouths the words silently, expressing deep
                 denial*]

NARRATOR   At that moment, the cock crowed. [*Peter falls to his knees.
                 Then he snuffs out the candle(s) or turns off the lantern.*]

                 —C.M.

25. Jesus? Oh, Yes, Jesus

John 18:38b–19:16

This exchange has been done many times in many ways. Here, I wanted to have some irony in the reflection, so I constructed the ending as I have done. The final sentence is actually a quote from Gandhi. It's true that Christianity is more than "an idea," but it seemed to fit here, and to add a touch of hope.

Production Notes

Participants: *Pilate, Jesus, Priest, Voice*

This is a combination of inner and outer dialogue. Pilate is reflecting on his encounter with Jesus while pieces of the encounter are played out. Pilate's outer dialogue is labeled with his name, while his inner dialogue is separated from the outer dialogue into paragraphs

PILATE   [*to audience*] Jesus? Oh, yes, Jesus. He was that ragtag little man with the piercing eyes. He was a religious fanatic whose "loyal" followers all vanished when he was caught. I remember when he first arrived, dirty, a bit scraped up, and as contemptible as are all Jews. He seemed so fragile in appearance, but turned out to be a gladiator in spirit.

JESUS   My kingdom is not of this world. If it were, my servants would fight to prevent my arrest by the Jews. But now my kingdom is from another place.

PILATE   [*to Jesus*] You are a king, then!

JESUS   You say that I am a king. In fact, I was born and came into the world to testify to the truth. Everyone on the side of truth listens to me.

PILATE   [*to Jesus*] What is truth? [*to audience*] He talked to me and yet not to me. I felt like he wanted me to see his perspective as if my life depended on it. He seemed more concerned for my well-being than his own. Like other fanatics, he had his own version of truth and thought that it was THE version. I have enough of gods who are emperors who change their minds every other week! I wish there was one God and one Truth. That would be something to die for!

PILATE   [*to audience*] People of Jerusalem. I find no case against this Jesus. But you have a custom that I release someone for you at the Passover. Do you want me to release for you the King of the Jews? [*to audience*] I hate Passover. Some ancient celebration based in the myth of these people. There is always some trouble every Passover. I thought this small encounter would be it and I would be done. But they called out "Free Barrabas!" Barrabas was a low-life thief. The pit of my stomach wrenched when I heard them want to release a leech like Barrabas and keep this man. What was he to them? So I had him flogged until his blood flowed down his back and onto the ground. It was not as gratifying an experience as

74.

it usually was. When I presented him to the crowd, their response to this man, now crippled with the beating, chilled even my bones. "Crucify him!," they yelled over and over again.

PILATE [*to audience*] Take him yourself and crucify him.

PRIEST We have a law that calls for his death because he claims to be the Son of God.

PILATE [*to audience*] That caught me by surprise. I was again chilled to hear those words.

PILATE [*to Jesus*] Where are you from, Jesus? [*pause*] Do you refuse to speak to me? Do you not know that I have the power to release you, and power to crucify you?

JESUS You would have no power over me unless it was given to you from above; therefore, the one who handed me over to you is guilty of a greater sin.

PRIEST Pilate, if you release this man, you are no friend of the emperor. Everyone who claims to be king, sets himself against the emperor.

PILATE [*to audience*] So that was it. This wily little weasel priest would use my own political reality against me. Of course, Caesar is god and king and will tolerate no other. Therefore, Jesus was a threat to the state. What a lot of donkey bray! But I was cornered. I could not now let this poor, bloodied man go.

PILATE [*to audience*] People, here is your king.

VOICE Away with him! Crucify him!

PILATE [*to audience*] Shall I crucify your King?

VOICE We have no king but Caesar!

PILATE [*to audience*] Yeah, right! They were willing to shout a bald-faced lie in order to have this man killed. They hated Caesar more than anything. If killing this man would prevent a riot, so be it. I handed him over with orders to be crucified. Though he was an impressive man in his own way, his religious movement ended with a whimper. He was a rare one, and I believe that, had his ideas ever caught on, such a one as he could have changed even the Roman Empire.

VOICE There is no army strong enough to defeat an idea whose time has come.

—K.H.

26. It Is Finished

John 19:16b-30

Production Notes

Participants: *Three readers*

This depiction of the crucifixion scene may be used as the final piece in a Tenebrae service, a special Good Friday worship event that uses the symbol of diminishing light to point to the death of the Light of World. After each "it is finished," lights may be dimmed, and candles extinguished. One possibility is to have background music softly playing something like Samuel Barber's "Adagio for Strings," "Were you There When They Crucified My Lord?" or another piece that conveys the grief of Good Friday. Pace the readings and pauses so that the reading times well with the music.

READER 1   Then he handed him over to them to be crucified. So they took Jesus; and carrying the cross by himself, he went out to what is called the Place of the Skull, which in Hebrew is called Golgotha. There they crucified him, and with him two others, one on either side, with Jesus between them. Pilate also had an inscription written and put on the cross. It read, "Jesus of Nazareth, the King of the Jews." Many of the Jews read this inscription, because the place where Jesus was crucified was near the city; and it was written in Hebrew, in Latin, and in Greek. Then the chief priests of the Jews said to Pilate,

READER 2   Do not write, "'The King of the Jews,'" but, "'This man said, I am King of the Jews.'"

READER 3   Then Pilate answered,

READER 1   What I have written I have written.

2&3   It is finished.

[*pause*]

READER 1   When the soldiers had crucified Jesus, they took his clothes and divided them into four parts, one for each soldier. They also took his tunic; now the tunic was seamless, woven in one piece from the top. So they said to one another,

READER 2   Let us not tear it, but cast lots for it to see who will get it.

READER 3   This was to fulfill what the scripture says, "They divided my clothes among themselves, and for my clothing they cast lots." And that is what the soldiers did.

READER 1   It is finished.

[*pause*]

READER 2   Meanwhile, standing near the cross of Jesus were his mother, and his mother's sister, Mary the wife of Clopas, and Mary Magdalene. When Jesus saw his mother and the disciple whom he loved standing beside her, he said to his mother, "Woman, here is your son." Then he said to the disciple, "Here is your mother." And from that hour the disciple took her into his own home.

READER 3   I am thirsty.

READER 1   It is finished.

—C.M.

27. Mary on Sunday Morning

John 20:1-18

We often miss the significance of the fact that Jesus appeared first to women, who then became the first evangelists. Once again, Jesus has defied society's status quo. Appearing to Mary, who once occupied the lower rungs of society, Jesus has raised her up to new heights. It is another sign that Jesus accepts all who seek him.

READER 1 Now Mary was used to being the talk of the town.

READER 2 Her history was, shall we say, colorful.

READER 1 We don't want to go into the gory details in front of the kids.

READER 2 But we can say that she shared space with demons.

READER 1 Not one, not two, not three, not four

READER 2 not five, not six

READER 1 but seven, count 'em, seven demons!

READER 2 Jesus was the one who cast out those devilish demons.

READER 1 Her life began again.

READER 2 Without the voices.

READER 1 In control again.

READER 2 Able to walk the streets with self-respect.

READER 1 A whole woman again.

READER 2 Not torn apart by demons.

READER 1 [*slower and more sober*] Now her savior…

READER 2 Her personal savior…

READER 1 Had died the most gruesome death.

READER 2 Her hope—gone.

READER 1 Her future—uncertain.

READER 2 So she went to the garden on the morning after Sabbath.

READER 1 The third day after his death.

READER 2 Into the garden, to the tomb.

READER 1 Where his cold corpse lay.

READER 2 [*pause, then surprise*] But, what is this! The tomb is empty, the body is gone.

READER 1 I knew I should have come earlier! They have taken him away!

READER 2 Beg your pardon, can I help?

READER 1 Oh sir, can you help? The Romans have come and moved the body of the man who was buried in this tomb. He was everything to me. Can you tell me where they have moved him?

Production Notes

Participants: *Two readers*

At the tomb scene, Reader 1 voices Mary's words, and Reader 2 plays Jesus. The pace in the first part is quick. The second part, at the tomb, is slower and more serious.

READER 2 They haven't moved him at all.

READER 1 Please don't make jokes. We, my friends and I, owe him everything. We all love him and miss him.

READER 2 Woman, why are you weeping. Who are you looking for?

READER 1 Sir, if you have carried him away, please tell me where you have laid him, and I will take him away.

READER 2 Mary!

READER 1 Oh! Rabbouni!

READER 2 Yes, Mary. But do not hold onto me, because I have not yet ascended to God. But go to my brothers and say to them that I am ascending to my Father and your Father, my God and your God.

READER 1 In her heart she said, "Jesus, I love you."

READER 2 And through the generations her love for Jesus has been a model for many generations of believers.

READER 1 Mary Magdalene, the first one to see our risen Lord.

READER 2 If such a one as she can be precious to Jesus, anyone can.

—K.H.

28. Faithing Thomas

John 20:19-31

Thomas is often portrayed negatively because of his doubting. However, it is his very lack of faith that doggedly forces him to pursue understanding. His doubt becomes the avenue leading him to the most profound of the disciples' proclamations: that Jesus is both Lord and God.

READER 1   [*in a stage whisper*] Locked, bolted, chained, barricaded, blocked, shut tight! The doors were locked for fear of the Jews.

READER 2   When whom to their wondering eyes should appear?

READER 1   A little sleigh with eight tiny reindeer?

READER 2   [*more than a little annoyed*] Noooo! Wrong season, wrong story.

READER 1   Then to who and to whom did there appear?

READER 2   Not to Thomas's eyes [*said in a tone of correction*]. He went off fishing, or something.

READER 1   Thomas missed out the first time.

READER 2   Just imagine as Jesus came and stood among them and said, "Peace be with you."

READER 1   He'd better have said *peace*, or something like that. I imagine they dropped their donuts to see him of all people.

READER 2   Thomas was sure missing out. They all made a pact to rush out and find him and tell him what they saw.

READER 1   They saw Jesus.

READER 2   He showed them his hands and his side. Then the disciples rejoiced when they saw the Lord.

READER 1   Jesus said to them again, "Peace be with you."

READER 2   That would help, right about now.

READER 1   Then Jesus sent them out. Unlocking the doors first, I suppose, saying, "As the Father has sent me, so I send you."

READER 2   When he had said this, he breathed on them and said to them, "Receive the Holy Spirit. If you forgive the sins of any, they are forgiven them; if you retain the sins of any, they are retained."

READER 1   But Thomas, need we tell you again, was not with them when Jesus came.

READER 2   Until that time, he was know as Tardy Thomas, or "Where are Youuuu, Thomas?"

READER 1   But once the disciples caught up to him and told him who they had seen, all he could say was,

Production Notes

Participants: *Two readers*

This piece contains some humor in its portrayal of Thomas wanting to touch Jesus' wounds.

READER 2   Unless I see the mark of the nails in his hands, and put my finger in the mark of the nails and my hand in his side, I will not believe.

READER 1   To which the other disciples said,

1 AND 2   E-ooow, you are gross!

READER 2   For a while after that he was called Touchy Thomas. But that name didn't really suit him.

READER 1   A week later his disciples were again in the house, and Touchy Thomas was with them.

READER 2   Although the doors were shut, Jesus did it again!

READER 1   Jesus came and stood among them and said, "Peace be with you."

READER 2   Truly an appropriate phrase if ever there was.

READER 1   Then he said to Thomas,

READER 2   I dare you, c'mon I dare you.

READER 1   No, that's not what he said. Jesus said to Thomas, "Put your finger here and see my hands. Reach out your hand and put it in my side. Do not doubt, but believe."

READER 2   All at once the rest of the disciples said, "Yes, that's it, we'll call him Doubting Thomas." And they all appeared rather proud of themselves.

READER 1   Then Thomas answered Jesus,

READER 2   [in a new a new voice] My Lord and my God! My Lord and my God!

READER 1   It's a shame that the name Doubting Thomas has stuck with him all these years.

READER 2   For he proclaimed what we did not.

READER 1   His doubt gave birth to faith.

—C.M.

29. Go Fish
John 21:1-14

Jesus' appearances after the resurrection must have been a sign of joy and hope to his followers. It is the joy and hope I believe we can all feel when we realize that Jesus is there when you least expect him.

NARRATOR	After these things, Jesus again showed himself to the disciples by the Sea of Tiberias.
NATHANIEL	[*looking around*] Where is that voice coming from?
PETER	Just play cards.
NATHANIEL	Its creepy though. [*looks at his hand*] I need a king. Don't we all. Go fish.
NATHANIEL	[*putting down his cards*] Good idea, let's go fishing.
NARRATOR	So Nathaniel and Peter and the other disciples went fishing.
NATHANIEL	[*looking around*] There's that voice again.
PETER	[*exasperated*] Will you concentrate on fishing!?
NARRATOR	They went out and got into the boat, but they caught nothing.
PETER	We have caught nothing.
NATHANIEL	It's no wonder. That voice is scaring all the fish. I know it's scaring me.
PETER	Enough with your voices. [*pauses and listens*] Now you have me hearing things.
NATHANIEL	No, it's a different voice. Look, that man on the shore is shouting at us. What's he saying?
PETER	He said "Cast your nets on the right side of the boat."
NARRATOR	Out of desperation they did as the stranger instructed them. They were not able to haul in the nets because there were so many fish.
NATHANIEL	I think that guy on the shore is throwing his voice. You know if I didn't know better, I'd say that was the Lord.
PETER	It is! I'm swimming ashore.
NATHANIEL	Whoa there, Pete! It's one thing to fish in your birthday suit, but don't you think you could put your shirt and pants on to go ashore.
NARRATOR	So Peter dressed and swam to the shore, which was about 100 yards away. Jesus, said to Peter, "Bring some of the fish you caught." Jesus had started a fire and had some fish and bread all ready to eat.
PETER	Come on Nate. Give some fish, Jesus wants fish. Can you believe it?

Production Notes

Participants: *Narrator, Nathaniel, and Peter*

This has a pace that signifies these are close friends. The scene begins with Nathaniel and Peter playing a card game called "Go Fish." Each has a large hand of cards. Nathaniel seems to be the only one who can hear the narrator's voice and is trying to figure out where it is coming from.

NATHANIEL   What, that he wants more fish?
PETER   No, that he is alive.
NATHANIEL   Are you sure it's him?
NARRATOR   Jesus invited them to breakfast. Then he took bread and gave it to them and did the same with the fish. This was now the third time that Jesus appeared to the disciples after he was raised from the dead.
NATHANIEL   Peter, could that be the voice of God?
PETER   Now that Jesus has risen from the dead, all things are possible.

—K.H.